THE SPORT
★ ★ ★ ★ *of* ★ ★ ★ ★
PRESIDENTS

Alexandra Kitty

THE SPORT
★ ★ ★ ★ *of* ★ ★ ★ ★
PRESIDENTS

 PRENDE

Prende Publishing

Las Vegas ◊ Chicago ◊ Palm Beach

Published in the United States of America by

Histria Books

7181 N. Hualapai Way, Ste. 130-86

Las Vegas, NV 89166 USA

HistriaBooks.com

Prende Publishing is an imprint of Histria Books. Titles published under the imprints of Histria Books are distributed worldwide.

Library of Congress Control Number: 2024931030

ISBN 978-1-59211-425-2 (softbound)
ISBN 978-1-59211-441-2 (eBook)

Contents

To my mother

Preface

I am a researcher by design: when I delve into a topic, I like to be thorough and look at all sides of an issue. My drive for knowledge leads me to some interesting places, and when I was looking at how the press covered U.S. presidents, I suddenly looked beyond the headlines and noticed something very *intriguing:* U.S. presidents didn't just golf: they used the sport for a variety of clever purposes. It isn't about exercise or optics; it is about something else entirely, and it was a topic that fascinated me enough to explore.

I am hardly the first person to see the link between golf and U.S. presidents, as the presidential version of the game has captured the imagination of many writers over the decades, but my interest stems from my attention to strategy. Canada also has golfing prime ministers, for instance, but their use of the game is nowhere near the level of sophistication or utility of their U.S. counterparts. A U.S. president must be a magician of some sort, and one who can simultaneously battle both internal and external actors with gravitas, but where do these magicians *practice* and refine their craft?

The answer was out on the links. Once I saw this interesting connection, I wanted to know much more: how did each president use golf to make it his own magic act? What else do these players have in common? What separates them and what ultimately unifies them? That is my thesis that I have explored here, but it is not the only thing to enjoy with this read.

This book is a gateway to understanding this very elite club from a different angle: how the game of golf became the definitive Sport of Presidents. So ingrained is the game that it is highly unlikely that a non-golfing candidate could win a presidential race: without the golf, the contender is at a catastrophic disadvantage, and after doing my homework on this fascinating topic, I would boldly state that without golf, a president has no core to strengthen his magic act. My intent is to open a new pathway of exploring the topic, without going into the minutiae of which kind of golf cart a leader drove in or list every golf course a president played.

I sought to know why golf became the definitive game of Commanders in Chief for generations, and what shocked me with the answers. I hope you also enjoy this singular journey as much as I did.

Alexandra Kitty

Chapter One
The Sport of Presidents

The U.S. presidency has been a symbol of power and has been the dream goal for most of its citizens as it represents victory, success, and the ability to change the world. It is idealism and pragmatism wrapped in a single position and one that is not given but earned through a grueling campaign. The presidency is the sign that you have not just arrived, but you are ready to deliver your vision that lasts long after you are gone. The job of Commander-in-Chief is seen as one that has gravitas that is all work and strategy, but even presidents need a diversion to help them focus and regroup whenever a national or global crisis proves to be vexing.

What is fascinating to note is the number of presidents who had the same pastime in common: golf. Regardless of personal background, education, or previous profession, the sport is a unifying theme. North or South, Democrat or Republican, those who have held the highest office are drawn to the same game time and again, regardless of the decade or social climate that defined their times.

So ingrained is the sport to the position that when George Herbert Walker Bush passed away in 2018, his love of the sport was part of the final tributes, along with his political legacy. As his son George W. Bush made mention of his golfing at the time:

> "He played [golf] fast so he could move on to the next event, to enjoy the rest of the day, to expend his enormous energy, to live it all," George W. Bush said. "He was born with just two settings: full throttle, then sleep."

The game goes deeper than a mere reflection of a president's leadership style. Bill Clinton's "golf buddy" was (and still is as of this writing) former Canadian Prime Minister Jean Chretien. The game has been a shrewd and quiet way to cultivate political alliances for more than one president as we will see. The sport also serves as a quiet showcase of each leader's strategic prowess, both the highs and the lows: Warren G. Harding came in third in the first annual Washington newspaper correspondents' tournament in 1921 (quipping "How good do I have to be to win?"), but by 1923, his fatigue on the course was seen as a sign that he was ill and nearing the end.

As the United States became an increasingly powerful and influential nation, the sport of golf seems to be a natural extension of the American presidency: the game represents something more than a mere escape from the pressure of the job. It is not just a way to unwind or escape the pressures of the job, but its symbolic function should never be underestimated. It signals to citizens and leaders abroad that the president has control and everything is under control. While presidents have all wildly differed in background, policy, style, temperament, mandate, popularity, and ideology, what is the common thread among them is the sport they play.

The link between the sport and the office has a long and storied tradition even before the days of Dwight D. Eisenhower, who was dubbed the Golf President, and whose passion transformed golf into the Sport of Presidents. Ever since Eisenhower made the pastime part of the mythos, including installing The White House Putting Green in 1954 and sometimes going into the White House with his spiked golf shoes, almost every president save for Jimmy Carter has been an avid, and often gifted golfer. While William Howard Taft was the first one in office who played the sport, he would hardly be the last.

Presidents have used the sport to more than just unwind or get their dose of outdoor exercise: they often can hold their own with professional golfers, and show the world their skills extend beyond the White House. Deals have been negotiated on the green as Lyndon B. Johnston was known to do. Alliances with other world leaders have been cultivated on the course, as Clinton had done adroitly during his time in office. For those jockeying for the rare opportunity to get the president's ear — the path to do it is not always in the Oval Office or a G20 Summit, but during a game of golf. The importance of the sport at the nation's highest office cannot be dismissed. When the Commander in Chief is riding high in the polls, the press often lavishes praise on his seeming leisure pursuits as footage of his game makes national headlines, but when the president becomes unpopular, the amount of coverage is often the same, yet reporters will chastise the president for his choice of pleasure over work. But in both cases, the stories run without questioning who else is on the course and what is happening behind the scenes.

Golf is the sport of choice for those who make the White House their office, home, and legacy. It is not tennis, trap shooting, or cycling that keeps the presidents active and powerful, but golf. While there is no shortage of pursuits a president can engage in to let off steam, golf is the constant for almost every person who has won the toughest of competitions.

But why does golf and a presidency go together, and how did it become the Sport of Presidents? While there are pragmatic reasons why golf has become the natural sport of choice, its place in political power is more complicated than it first appears. It is the game that takes place on a large landscape, and its strategic ways can turn a course into a map. It is a symbol of power, pragmatism, and learning to think far ahead and in the long term that makes the game a powerful tool for the most powerful of people. As we will see throughout the book, it is the club that is more powerful than the sword, and has been the silent partner of many presidents throughout the decades. While not every president was a good golfer, each who played it had used it as part of their political repertoire. Johnson managed to get the 1964 Civil Rights Act to pass through the Senate by playing golf with those senators who weren't likely to vote in favor of it. By the end of the game, he broke through another barrier until he reached his goal.

Golf is not the only way a president indirectly communicates with the people: from church attendance to the choosing of a White House pet, there are many subtle ways to send a message, yet golf is one of the most elegant ways of doing it. It can disarm opponents as it can build bridges with them. It can allay fears as much as criticism. It can also be a show of strength, fitness, and shrewdness with a single stroke.

And when the tenure is over, a president can hang up the clubs as Calvin Coolidge left his behind in the White House, while others, such as George W. Bush, continued to play years after his second term was over. The game paints a very different portrait for each one who held the office, and each president made the game his own.

Golf has always been more than a sign of status; for a president, it is part of the machine that keeps the country moving forward. While some presidents have used the sport as a photo op, what they have presented to the public was a sign of fitness and vigor; yet behind the scenes, the game has a deeper political purpose.

It can also be a place to quietly work with the inner circle as *Politico* noted for Joe Biden's first golf game as President on April 17, 2021:

> Joe Biden is playing his first round of golf as president Saturday at Wilmington Country Club in Delaware.

> Biden is golfing with Ron Olivere, the father-in-law of Biden's late son Beau, and adviser Steve Ricchetti, according to a pool report. In nearly three months as president, Biden has often spent weekends at home in Wilmington without holding public events.

> But while Biden worked the course, he made an interesting remark:

> In 2014, when he served as vice president, he said a presidential run could hurt his golf game.

> "If you want to keep your handicap in golf don't run for president. So, I expect strokes," Biden said, according to CNN. It was unclear if he was joking, CNN reported.

> It's not clear if Biden had his best round Saturday.

> "The course record is still intact," Biden said, smiling and quipping to reporters.

Yet golf often helps the office rather than hinders it.

Because of its power, a president can immerse in the game and enjoy it on many levels. As filmmaker Todd Phillips revealed in August 2016, former President Clinton surprised Phillips that he enjoyed the game in celluloid form:

> [He] was amused to learn the former president's favorite movie is 2007['s] golfing movie 'Who's Your Caddy?', which starred Outkast's Big Boi.

> He said: "[Clinton] is literally everything you heard about. He's so engaging, he looks you in the eye and talks to you about what he thinks you would be interested in.

"I was sitting next to him and he kept talking to me about movies, because — he didn't know who I was but — 'Here's a director'.

"I remember him telling me about how he loves comedies and he said the one film he loved [when he was flying] was 'Who's Your Caddy?', that was his favorite comedy.

"And he said, 'Have you ever seen it? I was like 'I actually haven't seen that movie.'"

The game personalizes the leader as it still sets the president apart. It can push through legislation, break impasses, and also show the human side of the president.

But the game can also serve other purposes, such as helping the fortunes of those who fell out of favor with the public. Former President Barak Obama boldly did for troubled golfer Tiger Woods in February 2013:

U.S. President Barack Obama played golf Sunday with Tiger Woods, the White House said.

Once the sport's dominant player before his career was sidetracked by scandal, Woods joined Obama at the Floridian, a secluded and exclusive yacht and golf club on Florida's Treasure Coast, where Obama is spending the long Presidents Day weekend. The two had met before, but Sunday was the first time they played together.

The move caused shockwaves, and yet had its own strategic logic to it:

The foursome also included Jim Crane, a Houston businessman who owns the Floridian and the Houston Astros, and outgoing U.S. Trade Representative Ron Kirk, a former mayor of Dallas, White House spokesman Josh Earnest said. Crane and Kirk also were part of Obama's foursome Saturday, the White House said.

Obama, an avid golfer, also received some instruction last Saturday and played a few holes with Butch Harmon, Woods's former swing coach.

It was a surprising, but potent show of confidence that was in tune with Obama's egalitarian leadership style. A simple game spoke more eloquently than a speech ever could. People should accept and forgive, and if a president has no qualms about it, then neither should they.

Journalists, columnists, and pundits have used the Sport of Presidents to read the signs, as the *New York Times* did in 1990:

> George Bush is going through the motions of recreation, grimly determined not to be held captive in the White House. His aides, knowing his stubborn side, do not press him to cut short his 25-day holiday, even though some believe that it would be more appropriate if Mr. Bush returned to Washington for more than brief visits, as he was to on Sunday. And they would prefer it if he stopped speaking to reporters about the chilling Persian Gulf crisis while sitting in his golf cart. "The President doesn't even seem to be having fun racing around the golf course," the official added. "It's almost as though he's on some driven mission."

But there had been a different reportage from the same newspaper in 1990:

> President Bush has become the ninth honorary member of the Royal and Ancient golf club, the club announced yesterday in St. Andrews, Scotland.

> Bush, a high handicap player who has said he likes to "hack" at the game when he has time, joins a trio of illustrious American golfers- Jack Nicklaus, Arnold Palmer, and Gene Sarazen — as honorary members of the home of golf.

Golf is seen as an omen of the president's deepest thoughts as well as the leader's own personal prowess. Those insiders who know the president are often on the course, and they know much of the workings of the office go beyond the Oval Office and out in the field.

This book chronicles how each president made the sport their own, how they incorporated it into their political strategy, how the press interpreted their game, and the lasting impact of the game on the nation. It is one of the most underappreciated aspects of the American presidency, but like a swing of a club, the sport has moved the tiniest of grains to create a global powerhouse, allowing each Commander in Chief to facilitate critical deals, cultivate strategic alliances, and make bridges in impossible places on the path to progress. It is one of the most important sports in the history of the world, and it should not be any surprise it is the sport of choice of presidents. Its power is exciting as it is historical, and it has quietly, yet dutifully served the country one swing at a time. It is the sport that is most in tune with the soul of the highest office, and it is one whose role has not been fully appreciated.

This book is an empirical psychological odyssey of a different sort. Let's begin by taking a look at how the sport became so integral to the office in the first place.

Chapter Two
The Beginnings of a Natural Link

Anyhow, President Taft can still play golf.

— From the *Chicago Day Book*, November 6, 1912.

The game has been linked to the highest office for well over a century, pushing out tennis as the sport favored by those in office. As a visual demonstration of a leader's political strategy, no sport is as revealing or symbolic. It is slow, methodical, and dynamic. There are conscious and overt signs a player wishes to express on the green, but there are unconscious and covert signs to read to see the innermost workings of the most powerful player in the nation.

While we can look at golf from a traditional analytical perspective, it is more important to look through a lens of emotional literacy: what *feelings* does the structure of the game evoke? Bravery? Confidence? Cunning? Sociality?

With golf, the same game in the hands of a different president conjured vastly different psychological calling cards. Each imprinted something *different* to the mythos of the game. People do not vote by comparing political platforms, doing their research, looking for facts, reason, or empirical evidence: they vote by *feel,* or in rarer cases, the instinct for survival. A photograph of a president sitting at the desk of the Oval Office doesn't give the same insight as to the Commander in Chief's conduct out on the green. Where is the focus? What is the strategy? What are the results?

Golf is the reliable barometer of a president's fortunes, and it is instructive to look at the first golfing president who began one of the most important psychological benchmarks of the top player in the White House.

William Howard Taft, the 27th president, was the first of many to openly partake in the sport when he took office in 1909. He began a trend that still shows no signs of abating. While William McKinley was technically the first president who golfed, he kept his passion out of the press, though he wasn't always successful at keeping it a secret.

The *Washington Times* noted his playing on August 7, 1899:

> It the "chief" who has been taking notice of President McKinley as he plays golf at Lake Champlain, holds the mirror up to nature to get a proper focus of the distinguished stateman's "slouch hat, knickerbockers, and gay plaid stockings," the question is what do the possessors of kinetoscope cameras mean by losing the chance of their lives? A series of Mr. McKinleys in Sunday supplement colors would offer a refreshing change to the patrons of the social page. ... It Is no novelty for Mr. McKinley to see himself as others see him, via the daily press, but he has yet to experience the thrill of viewing his ego in the garb of a golfer and a golfer, at that, who, while he plays that most exasperating game, preserves an expression that is described as "benign."

The *New York Sun* also made a mention on November 25, 1906:

> Joel W. Burdick of Albany enjoys the distinction of having played in the first and only game of golf with President McKinley...

He played with those in his inner circle, as the August 6, 1897 edition of the New York Tribune noted to readers, yet still downplayed his involvement:

> As soon as the parade had ended the President, the Vice-President and the Secretary of War started for the golf links. They enjoyed a walk through the woods, and Vice-president Hobart and General Alger tried their hands at hitting a golf hall with golf sticks, President McKinley meanwhile looking on at their attempts.

And there was an interesting excuse for the golf-playing, according to the *Birmingham Age-Herald* on August 20, 1899:

> Since President McKinley went into golf by the advice of his physician, who thinks the president should be lighter by twenty pounds, it is quite the thing to golf off one's fat. The President's golf club plays over links

that cover only three miles, as a three-mile run, with accompanying exercise with the golf sticks, is enough for a puffing beginner.

McKinley had downplayed his sport of choice. Taft, on the other hand, was the game's passionate advocate who did it out in the open. And when he did, it was seen as newsworthy.

Taft was seen as a trend-setter, gracing the April 4, 1909 front page of the New York Tribune playing the game, with the headline, *Mr. Taft Revives the Popularity of Golf at the National Capital.* His picture was placed amid John D. Rockefeller and Andrew Carnegie. His love of the game was front-page news. If the nation's wealthiest men played, and the president played, then there was no question: golf was the sport: the one of power, prestige, skill, and the very symbol that one has arrived.

The *Los Angeles Herald* was aligned with the sentiment three days earlier on April 1, 1909 in an article headlined, *Athletics Fashions Set by Presidents: Tennis yields to golf as Taft succeeds Roosevelt,* with the added subtitle, "Strenuous Executive Caused National Revival of Almost Forgotten Sport, and Present Administration is Watched Anxiously." With Taft, the meaning of the sport transformed from passé pastime to a newsworthy pursuit of a winner. With a single presidency, a sport changed its very meaning.

It is not as if everyone approved of the president having golf as an outlet for stress, however, particularly as his presidency wore on. The *Seattle Republican* had harsh words for him and the sport he played in their November 8, 2012 edition:

President Taft played golf while the Republican party was being roasted and Nero of old fiddled while Rome burned. Is this history repeating itself?

Taft's association with golf was strong, and part of his persona. As the *Bluefield Evening Leader* let their readers know on April 23, 1909, playing the game was integral to getting close to the president:

Senator Jonathan Bourne, Jr., of Oregon, who is looked upon as a strong probability for President Taft's "golf cabinet," has called several times at the White House since the inauguration. As yet however, he and the president have not had a game of golf together, owing to Mr. Taft's being kept in the White House by pressure of work.

At Hot Springs, Va., and Augusta Ga. The senator was Mr. Taft's favorite golf companion. Bourne is a good man to play with. An expert player himself he always encourages his companion. Besides, the senator is always in a good humor and never wants to talk politics while the game is in progress.

When and where Taft played golf was the fodder for major news articles. Where would Taft play golf in New England? The *Newport Daily Press* had a detailed article July 17, 1910 accompanied by photographs of the President in action, as well as a long and detailed discussion of his game:

> If present plans are carried out President Taft will devote the major portion of a prolonged vacation to playing golf amid the New England hills. President Taft plays golf at all seasons of the year and in every variety of weather, but it is in the summer — when feels himself truly entitled to a vacation — that he derives the keenest enjoyment from the Skotch game.

It wasn't as if Taft was a monomaniac, but as he rose to power, one pursuit overtook the others, as the article went on to note:

> It is not too much to say that golf is entitled to pre-eminent place as President Taft's special hobby, having taken this foremost position since the Chief Magistrate has been introduced to the charms of the golf courses along the favored "North Shore" of Massachusetts Bay. Not that the athletic heavyweight President has allowed his increasing fondness for golf to entirely supplant his other favored diversions, horseback riding, and motorcycling, but unquestionably it enjoys the greatest prestige of the three.

The *New York Times* kept meticulous records of his golfing and added to the myth of the sport of presidents. When he played a game "in soaking rain," the March 28, 1909 story chronicled the last sopping details. His Vice President was his partner playing against General Clarence Edwards and Captain Archie Butt. When New York state politician Richard Croker paid the president a visit in Washington on April 5 of that same year, the Times noted they played together on the links. When in September he was so busy on his last day visiting one city, he had no golf, the Times relayed the message to readers. His wins, losses, and all his golfing factoids were presented regularly in the Paper of Record.

His involvement in the game did not go unnoticed in Canada. As the June 29, 1911 edition of the *Toronto Globe* noted in its headline: Senator Gallinger, the Canadian, Getting Desperate — President Taft Not Worrying, but is Playing Golf. While there was a critical vote happening, the article noted that while "this was going on, President Taft was playing a game of golf and refusing to worry."

Taft paid "high tribute to golf" another *Globe* article decree in its January 4, 1918 article, several years after he was no longer president:

Addressing himself to the devotees of Scotland's ancient game, Mr. Taft said:

"A man who plays golf and enjoys it must have a love for freedom and a spirit of independence. Such personal traits prompt one to play the game to the end. That is what we must do in this war. We must fight it through to victory and win the game at the eighteenth hole if it be necessary to play it through."

Golf was the allegory to the Great War: golf had the same strategies and required the same intellectual and moral qualities, according to the former president.

So how did golf become an integral part of presidential life? Its origins and presence in the White House began with Taft's integral association with it — as he reached for the highest mountain, it was golf that spoke to him, giving him his quiet time, as it also helped him in his presidential undertakings. It was a strong part of his identity from the start of his presidency, and the link came from it.

Taft was a robust, athletic man, and yet of everything he could do, golf became his greatest asset. Others could see him at play — and that so many people chose to watch him out on the green, much to his chagrin, it was the way Americans began to identify with him, as the game made him seem powerful, and more importantly, human.

Woodrow Wilson followed Taft, and also played golf, even as he was governor, even as he received important news, as the *Cairo Bulletin* recounted on June 26, 1912:

Gov. Woodrow Wilson was playing golf here when word reached him this afternoon of the selection of Judge Parker as temporary chairman of the Democratic national convention. He declined to discuss the result of the polling with newspaper men.

Yet the idea of presidents and golf was cemented in this unusual way in the *Washington Herald* on September 27, 1910:

Dr. Woodrow Wilson was playing golf when he heard the news of his nomination. Golf, be it remembered, is the pastime of Presidents.

It would not be the last time Wilson made headlines by the mere fact that he was playing the game. Headlines such as *Wilson Plays Golf* were not unheard of during his tenure, as it was in the *Richmond Times-Dispatch* on November 15, 1914, which also noted his "exceptionally good score," even if he was "not familiar with the links."

President Warren G. Harding would take up the mantle, as he was photographed on the links throughout his tenure as well, from Kansas to New Jersey to Florida, and he was known to play the game two to three times a week. When he was out in Palm Beach playing a game one March 25, 1922 article stated with approval that even "a few days of southern sun served to tinge his face and hands with tan." He was even photographed repairing his golf bag. By Harding, there was no doubt that the sport of presidents would be golf for generations to come. Three presidents in a row who could pick up a club and instantly gain more than newspaper attention, but also command respect as they became relatable to the average citizen: even presidents needed downtime, and bothered to repair their own golf bags.

But why do U.S. presidents seem to own the game of golf? It is not as if other world leaders aren't linked to the sport, yet it was Taft who brought the sport front and center. When congressmen or senators needed to seek a presidential audience, they went to play a game with him — and many of those games were covered by the press. Who was in the president's good books? One need not look any further than the links. It gave many clues to how bills and policies were passing along — or weren't, as we will see in later chapters. When generals played with the president, it sent signals to others about what was transpiring on the war front. When a president played, it often showed that he was confident in the process and of his own abilities, that he needn't fret away in private in the Oval Office: he could be playing a round, knowing his leadership would bring what he deemed optimal for his people.

Taft astutely used the game to show his leadership abilities and coolness under pressure. Wilson showed his prowess by taking on courses that were unfamiliar to him, proving to voters and the press that he could handle a novel situation with ease, even in the snow. Harding was seen in numerous photo ops enjoying the game, usually with others playing with him, signaling he was at ease with being out in public. Each man made the sport relay a specific message to make it his own.

But they would hardly be the only presidents to pick up a club to send a message to the public or use it to ensure their vision for the nation went through as planned.

Chapter Three
The Exclusive Club

Not every president who ruled in the last century golfed. Jimmy Carter, for instance, was one of the few presidents in modern times who did not partake in the sport at all.

After Harding, three presidents were not golfers: Calvin Coolidge, Herbert Hoover (who avoided the game given his tenure during the Great Depression), and Harry S. Truman.

Yet the press was hopeful that Coolidge was about to pick up the mantle. The *Washington Evening Star* seemed to imply it could be a real possibility on July 31, 1927, and one significant section was headlined May Start Golf:

> President Coolidge has been giving outward evidence of late that he may be considering taking up golf while out here on his vacation. For the last three evenings while out horseback riding he has ridden to the nine-hole golf course, laid out up in the hills about a mile and a half away from the lodge, where he dismounted and walked about the grounds while he has been studying the layout. To those who have inquired whether or not he has been contemplating playing golf, he has replied in the negative.

> At any rate, he inquired of one of the members of his party yesterday about the golf course in the hills, but he added that he was asking out of curiosity and not because of any intention on his part, to play. However, those who are familiar with the President's tactics say that this is the way he generally maneuvers before he does something out of the ordinary and that his secret visit to the court...

Even a maybe to golf was considered a newsworthy topic of discussion. Coolidge did have a set of golf clubs, and he played occasionally, yet he was not closely associated with the game or had it as part of his persona.

However, Franklin D. Roosevelt did golf before contracting polio in 1921, long before becoming president. His college days showed promise as an able golfer, becoming the club champion at Campobello Island Golf Club in New Brunswick in 1900. While he did not play golf while in office, golf was not far from his mind, however: as he funded many public works projects, creating municipal golf courses during his tenure, yet while he fostered the game while in office, he could not take up the sport as president, and it seemed as if the sport took a prolonged hiatus, even as Truman became president and was not a golfer.

And then came Ike.

While the previous four presidents shied away from the sport, there were those whose identity was deeply linked to the game, such as Dwight D. Eisenhower who was dubbed the Golf President by the press. He played the game daily, using the South Lawn, brought in a 3,000 square foot putting green outside the Oval Office, and his love of the game brought back the link between the presidency and the game, as one UPI article entitled Eisenhower Is First Golfer Since Harding on March 5, 1953, noted at length:

> President Eisenhower's enthusiasm for golf is remindful of that fact we haven't had a golf-lover in the White House since Warren G. Harding.
>
> …[Former President Ulysses S.] Grant is believed to have been the first president ever to see a golf game. He commented: "It looks like good exercise, but what's the little white ball for?"
>
> Harding-up to the present — was our most eager golfing chief. He found in golf a chance to relax. He usually made small bets with his opponents, sometimes on each hole. His caddies used to try to give the boss a lift by throwing his ball out of the rough or traps, but Harding would throw the ball back. He wanted to play fair.

At first, the revelation was celebrated, and there were copious references to his playing throughout his tenure. He even held more than one Press Conference in the same place where he was golfing. Any tidbit relating to the president's love of the sport was fair game for the press — even when he was parting with something for charity, as the June 17, 1953 edition of the *Dunn Daily Record* noted:

> A pair of President Eisenhower's spiked golf shoes is bound for Korea.

Nearly a half-ton of clothing was rounded up Friday by the White House staff to be sent to Korean war victims. The collection included trousers, socks, shirts, and golf shoes from the president and four dresses from Mrs. Eisenhower.

When he was criticized for playing the game, and he played more than 800 rounds during his presidency, there was the press to come to his defense as the May 2, 1959 edition of the *Detroit Tribune* did in one piece:

We doubt also that a nonpartisan survey would show

PRESIDENT EISENHOWER'S GOLF

has any close relation to unemployment. However well-intentioned they may be, we question if the union leaders who deal in such charges are the best representatives of the unemployed. They work a far shorter week than the President — who even on golfing vacations has to take work with him.

It was acknowledged that playing golf on the job was not play or leisure, and his devotion to the game was not seen as an impediment to his presidential duties. The sport was not a pastime, but an integral part of the job.

But the consensus was not unanimous. The *New York Times* saw it differently in an April 19, 1953 article:

President Eisenhower's fondness for golf, including practicing iron shots on the White House lawn and last week's outing on the links of the Augusta (Ga.) National Golf Club, is the mild sort of revolt all Presidents stage against the confinement of their job — now probably the greatest burden placed on any human in the world.

But the notion that golf was linked to the job, and not away from it began to form.

No detail wasn't newsworthy when it came to the sport of presidents. If the president was unhappy with his playing, it made news, such as it did in the February 28, 1953 edition of the *Key West Citizen*:

Eisenhower, reportedly disappointed about his golf game, fixed his sights on a score in the 80s today and got ready to welcome Bobby Jones — an old friend who made of history.

Eisenhower, vacationing over the week end at the Augusta National dub, arranged to turn over to Jones a portrait of the golfer which the President painted.

Jones, unable to golf because of a back ailment, was scheduled to arrive from Atlanta late this afternoon. He will receive the painting from Eisenhower at the club house.

Eisenhower is living at the golf course in Jones' white frame cottage. The President flew here from Washington Thursday and will return tomorrow. Eisenhower spent a good part of the day on the links yesterday and was said to have heed somewhat chagrined about his score...

And when bad weather prevented the president from golfing, the public was sure to hear about it, as the April 14, 1954 edition of the *Chapel Hill Daily Record* informed readers with an article with the headline, *Weather Keeps Ike From Golf:*

Damp weather and a pile of paper work kept President Eisenhower off the golf course this morning, but he planned to try his skill at the Augusta National during the afternoon.

The chief executive went to work in his tiny office over the professional's shop at the club at 8 a. m. and during the course of the morning.

When he was meeting directly with the press, he was not giving up his golf game, as the *United Press* told readers on August 4, 1953:

President Eisenhower has been playing golf usually on the afternoon of his news conference day, Wednesday. He doesn't knock off work for the entire afternoon, however. He usually returns to his office and sign papers prepared by staff aides in his absence or confers with top advisors.

His post-golf activities often mean late-breaking news at the White House, too. As a result, wives of White House staff aides and reporters are getting accustomed to their husbands being late for dinner on Wednesdays.

Eisenhower rarely took orders from anyone — yet it was his Secret Service agent Deeter B. Flohr who was a rare bird who drew the line and made sure the President didn't cross it, as he told the *New York Times* on November 25, 1963:

> Only the close relationship of the two men and General Eisenhower's fondness for the big agent could result in the incident that occurred one day on Augusta National Golf Course. General Eisenhower had badly topped a tee shot and became so enraged that Mr. Flohr grew alarmed. The President's face was discolored and the veins of his neck became rigid.
>
> Mr. Flohr commanded the President to "stop that." He told the President to get into the electric cart or he would pick him up bodily and carry him back to the clubhouse.

Golf had to be factored into everything Eisenhower did: it was a daily presence and cemented the sport to the White House. There would no longer be a long gap of presidents who did not golf while in office, and for the exception of the aforementioned Carter, every president since Eisenhower would take up the sport of presidents.

John F. Kennedy was also a golfer, who played on the Harvard golf team, and was an able one at that, and until 2016, was considered the best presidential golfer. Despite his physical limitations, he was a superior golfer, though because of his presidential campaign and the optics of seeming too aristocratic in the public eye (see Chapter Five), he was forced to keep a low profile while on the links.

Yet his golfing prowess was still a strong part of his legacy: Cuban premier Fidel Castro challenged Kennedy to a game of golf in 1961, expressing confidence that he could beat him. Castro had at first mocked Eisenhower for playing the sport, decreeing that the former president was "incapable of governing and could only play with the little ball," but soon after, used the sport as a photo op to show his own abilities on the links. For all the derision, Castro was envious enough to preen in front of the cameras on something where the then-current U.S. president reigned supreme, and others before him dominated with passion.

Not that he did not have a mishap while playing office. He made news April 6, 1961, when he caused an unintentional injury according to the *Globe and Mail*:

The White House confirmed today that President John F. Kennedy beaned a Secret Service man with a wild shot at Palm Beach, Fla., Monday. The man wasn't hurt.

Press Secretary Pierre Salinger told reporters he did not know whether the ball was a hook or a slice, but reports from Palm Beach earlier indicated Mr. Kennedy was hooking some shots that day.

Yet when other diplomats and world leaders played golf, they were likened to Kennedy, as the Globe and Mail did n 1962. Kennedy had held an hour-long chat on "international matters" with Eisenhower in 1962 at the El Dorado Country Club's golf course. When he vacationed at Hyannis Port, golf was always on the agenda. Though he was less ostentatious with regards to the game, it was a powerful tool in his repertoire.

He had played with Reverend Billy Graham, who had later recounted a fateful turn to the *New York Times* in 1971:

The first time I became suspicious that the United States might become involved in Indochina was in January, 1961. I had just played golf with President-elect John Kennedy. Sitting in the clubhouse afterward, Mr. Kennedy was making observations on a number of domestic and foreign problems that he would immediately face upon becoming president in a few days.

When Kennedy was assassinated in 1963, his mother Rose was delivered the grim news as she herself was playing the game at the Hyannis Port Golf Club.

Lyndon B. Johnson was savvy enough to see the sport as a means to his political ends (See Chapter Nine). He frequented Burning Tree, and though one golf pro in 1966 said Johnson was on the "bottom" of a list of presidential golfers as he lacked a "zest" for it; however, Johnson was not so much about using the game to relax, but to get his agenda push through by making deals out on the links.

Yet his golf-playing made frequent headlines in the press. In 1967, he quipped that he gave up drinking, and took up golf as its replacement. The New York Times quipped, "This is alarming, if true, for in the present state of the world and the Presidency it really should be the other way around." In April 1964, his rumored playing of the game caused media speculation, and the question was put to then-White House Press Secretary George E. Reedy who confirmed it:

"He walked around nine holes with some friends," Mr. Reedy said.

Mr. Reedy said that the last time he recalled Mr. Johnson playing golf was in 1960 at Palm Beach, Fla. when he visited President-elect Kennedy.

Richard Nixon has an uneven relationship with the game, first taking up the sport when he served as Eisenhower's Vice President, and eventually building a three-hole course at his home. He was never known to relax while playing, however, and when his second presidential term began to unravel, he gave up the game entirely. For Nixon, his game greatly reflected his own troubled presidency.

Yet he played with the Reverend Billy Graham and for Christmas 1967, Nixon gave him four clubs:

> "While vacationing in Europe, I played golf with some friends and Ruth loved to walk around looking for golf balls, always coming back with a sackful! I played some of the best golf I have ever played with those rented clubs, and tried to buy them from the golf professional, who would not sell them. Weeks later I told my friend and often golf partner Richard Nixon how much I had enjoyed playing with those Tony Lema Golf Clubs. To my utter surprise, the next Christmas (1967), those golf clubs showed up as a gift from him! I don't know how in the world he ever managed it but he did."

Gerald Ford has an interesting conundrum as a golfing president: he was seen as both physically inept at times, thanks to a few publicized errant swings, yet he was an able golfer who would be the first Commander in Chief to be a member of the USGA, and in 1994, was an honorary chairman of the President's Cup (See Chapter Fourteen for an in-depth discussion). He was an underdog who was working hard and trying his best, and his golfing seemed to prove it, according to one August 1976 *New York Times* piece:

> It may have been the rarified air. President Ford's drives soared farther than normal on the golf course. His serves had more zing on the tennis court. And in politics as well, after nine days of campaign strategy planning at 8,200 feet above sea level in the Rockies, he seemed free of the gravitational pull of reality. The underdog President thought he could win.

Yet five golf trips courtesy from a United States Steel Corp.'s lobbyist got him bad publicity. Other times, it was his forgetfulness that got him in the media's bad books, as the time he forgot his golf clubs back in the White House when he wished to play at the Burning Tree Country Club on August 26, 1974. His wayward swing was a danger to youth, as one June 25, 1974 article decreed when he was still the country's Vice President:

> [Ford] struck a spectator in the head as he teed off yesterday at Duff's Celebrity Golf Tournament.
>
> The spectator, 17-year-old Tom Gerard of south Minneapolis, was taken to hospital and later released after doctors determined he had suffered only a minor bump on the head. The Vice-President was unaware of the mishap until informed by aides later during the golf match.

It was not the only incident of the day:

> There was a second near accident later in the game when Mr. Ford, teeing off on the 16th hole, hit a golf cart carrying a policeman. The officer was not injured.

Even after his presidency, during a Bob Hope Desert golf tournament, he hit two spectators in the first round of the game. While he was an able golfer, it was his missteps that most people remembered.

Ronald Reagan was not as avid a golfer as some others in the exclusive club, yet he was serious enough about the sport to take lessons from Max Elbin, who had taught five other presidents, including Eisenhower, the game. His most famous golfing anecdote came on October 21, 1983, when he played at the Augusta Country Club when "an armed man crashed the gates, took hostages and demanded to talk to Reagan." Though the gunman was arrested within moments, it was a shocking ordeal. According to his White House diary for that fateful day, the president took it in stride:

> I taped my Sat. radio bit & we left for Augusta Ga. We all stayed in the Eisenhower cottage at Augusta Country Club—home of the Masters golf tourney. There were the Shultzs, the Don Regans & the Nick Bradys. We turned out to be a fun group. Dinner at the Club then home to bed. About 4 A.M. or so I was awakened by Bud McFarlane. I joined him & George S. in the living room. We were on the phone with Wash.

about the Grenada situation. I've OK'd an outright invasion in response to a request by 6 other Caribbean nations including Jamaica & Barbados. They will all supply some forces so it will be a multi-national invasion. Finally back to bed for a short while & then up for golf. I was better than at Andrews but still not good. I guess you have to play more than 4 times in almost 3 yrs. We reached the 16th hole and suddenly were stopped. A man with a gun was holding hostages in the golf shop demanding to talk to me. I got on the car phone & tried 5 times to talk to him but he always hung up on me. Dave F. was a hostage but talked his way out on the grounds that he could get the message to me. Lanny Wiles remained a hostage for almost 2 hours before he made a break & got away. One by one the hostages got away one way or another. The gun man was taken into custody. Meanwhile we had taken a back road & reached Eisenhower cottage. And so to bed—after a pleasant dinner.

George Herbert Walker Bush was not only an avid golfer and "speed golfer", but George 41's family legacy is firmly entrenched in the game (see Chapter Ten for a detailed discussion). On his mother's side, his grandfather George Herbert Walker became the president of the USGA (the United States Golf Association) as was his father, former senator Prescott Bush, and Walker founded the Walker Cup.

His father had golfed with Eisenhower, and when he passed away, the October 9, 1972 obituary in the *New York Times* had highlighted his association:

He was a confidant and frequent companion of President Eisenhower on the links, mixing putts with politics. A reporter who once asked the Senator about his golfing experiences with the President was told: "Nobody who plays golf with the President ever talks about it. Any other questions?"

Mr. Bush, in fact, was an excellent golfer. He was the national senior golf champion in 1951, when, at the age of 56, he shot an 18-hole score of 66. He was president of the United States Golf Association in 1935 and eight times the champion of the Round Hill Club in Greenwich.

Bush's then-Vice President Dan Quayle was often ridiculed for his various gaffes, yet he, too was an excellent golfer, yet the *New York Times* had its own snarky take in a December 22, 1988, Op-Ed piece:

> Still, Bush scattered the plums around: the moderates got most of them, the conservatives got Sununu and Kemp and the golfers got Quayle.

Yet with the President, golf was a way for other politicians to get an audience with him as one May 1, 1990, *New York Times* article recounted:

> Senator Don Nickles of Oklahoma is one of many conservative Republicans who said he had been invited to the White House more often than under Mr. Reagan. "I'm a golfer, so he had me to a get-together with Lee Trevino," Mr. Nickles said. "No question about it — this helps in relations."

His game would be the source of criticism three months later in the same paper that blared in its headlines that the president looked "grim" golfing:

> "It looks horrible," one Bush adviser said of the scenes of the President fishing and golfing and running, juxtaposed with others of frightened families of the Americans detained in Iraq and Kuwait and the frightened families of troops leaving for the Middle East.

> "The President doesn't even seem to be having fun racing around the golf course," the official added. "It's almost as though he's on some driven mission."

The optics of an unhappy golfer would be the beginnings of voter discontent, and Bush would lose the following presidential race to another avid golfer who looked happy as he played the sport.

Bill Clinton was well-known for his love of the game, and when he was elected, the press had high hopes for the game, as the *Globe and Mail* did January 20, 1993:

> Bill Clinton — President Clinton as of this afternoon- is an avid golfer. The evidence is that he will bring to the White House an interest in golf deeper than any president since Dwight D. Eisenhower from 1952 to 1960. His level of interest can be gauged from a letter he wrote Nov. 24 to Robert Trent Jones Jr. at his office in Palo Alto, Calif.

The letter is on stationery out of the National Campaign Headquarters in Little Rock, and was passed on here through Jones's office. It's tongue-in-cheek, but shows that Clinton enjoys golf.

"Dear Bob," Clinton addressed the architect, who designed the Chenal Country Club in Little Rock where Clinton has played much of his golf recently. "Why don't you design a par 85 course for the White House lawn? That would signify real dedication to the Clinton administration. Thanks for everything."

Yet he used the sport to carefully cultivate relationships with other world leaders. He was noted for playing golf with then Canadian Prime Minister Jean Chretien, and the men stayed friends long after their respective terms were over. They both had a love for the game, and their mutual sport served as a starting point for both their private fraternization — and their political work.

As the April 29, 2000 edition of the *Globe and Mail* recounted:

Prime Minister Jean Chrétien will play a round of golf with U.S. President Bill Clinton today during a weekend visit to Washington.

Canadian officials say Mr. Clinton invited Mr. Chrétien to join him for a game when he learned the Prime Minister was on a private visit to the U.S. capital.

The two have played golf several times, but Mr. Chrétien has always refused to say who won.

Mr. Clinton, the longer hitter, likes to putter around the course, kibbitzing with his partners and offering up tips, according to a former diplomat who has played with both of them. Mr. Chrétien is strictly business. He likes to play fast, waiting impatiently through Mr. Clinton's endless practice swings. He isn't crazy about unsolicited advice.

They would continue to be associated as a golfing pair, particularly in the Canadian media, that always yearned for acceptance from U.S. presidents. Clinton's golfing with their leader was reassuring and gave the press something to brag about to readers back home.

Yet it wasn't positive press that kept the two men together. In fact, the two had played together in August 2017, which the former Prime Minister recounted in an October 14, 2018 piece in the *Toronto Star*:

> On the other hand, with a partner like Bill Clinton, the day becomes truly memorable. I was up at six o'clock, and at seven I was driving along Highway 55 towards Sherbrooke. I arrived at the golf club at 9:30, the time we'd arranged. I was told that Clinton would be late, and I thought to myself that we would probably start the game at around eleven o'clock, because I knew his habits, and that's exactly when he arrived.

In a 2018 public conversation, Chretien emphasized the golf:

> 'We were good friends,' Chretien continued, 'We played golf... We had very few problems. We had problems, everybody has problems, but we tried to solve them. And we'd talk about it. And you had to make concessions and I had to make concessions, but we had in mind what was best for our countries and trust is everything. We didn't try to score political points. I didn't want to take advantage of my friendship.'

In an April 5, 2018, *Globe and Mail* article, the relationship was noted once again:

> It has been almost 15 years since Mr. Chrétien was prime minister, but some Canadians may remember the numerous times he picked up his clubs to join former U.S. president Bill Clinton for a round. The president loved the game as much as the prime minister and they played together frequently during their overlapping years in office from 1993 to 2001. In Mr. Clinton's memoir, he referred to Mr. Chrétien as "a strong ally, confidant, and frequent golfing partner."

Clinton endeared himself to his Northern neighbors, and the goodwill remains strong to the present, with his golf games with Chretien as being fondly remembered by the Canadian press, years after he already left office. The images on the links endured far longer than any policy, deal, or legislation associated with him in his eight years in the White House. One of his final images as president showed how dedicated he seemed to the game as one 2001 *Golf Digest* article began:

> There was a touching photograph last weekend portraying President Clinton in a chaotic Oval Office cluttered with packing wrap and boxes.

Off to one side, leaning against his desk, was a putter and what appeared to be a wedge.

George W. Bush, or George 43, is also an avid golfer but had kept his public outings to a minimum after the September 11, 2001, terrorist attacks. Here, sacrificing the game was a symbol in itself as he confessed in 2008:

"I didn't want some mom whose son may have recently died to see the commander in chief playing golf," he said.

"I feel I owe it to the families to be in solidarity as best as I can with them. And I think playing golf during a war just sends the wrong signal."

He did make exceptions — when he played with his father and former President, as he did in June 2003:

President Bush, joined by his father, hit a cool, damp golf course early Sunday, pulling up in a golf cart to the first tee and exclaiming "Happy Father's Day."

Former President Bush went first and without hesitation drove the ball down the fairway. "No mulligans," he said, refraining from taking another shot.

The game was seen as a touching moment between father and son:

President Bush opened a long weekend of golf and fishing Friday by hooking his first drive into a riverbank. He found his stroke on his second try, cheered by his father, who proclaimed it a "good ball!"

And the family ties that May also took place on the links:

For the second day in a row, President Bush said he wasn't going to take reporters' questions on the golf course. Then, he made an exception. "Yes, I talked to my mother."

And how was she on Mothers' Day morning? "Slightly sleepy but appreciative," the president said of his phone conversation with former first lady Barbara Bush.

For the younger George Bush, his game showed the link to his family, while he carefully downplayed his pursuit as a sign of sensitivity to the families of soldiers fighting in a war.

Barack Obama took up golf in 1997 on the advice of his wife Michelle as his previous sport — basketball — was proving too taxing on him. His game improved while in office, and numerous reports had noted the upward trajectory. His game was symbolic of his presidency. As the August 8, 2014 edition of the *Boston Globe* noted during one stay at Martha's Vineyard:

> Over the next 15 days — the longest summer vacation of his presidency — he'll go out to eat several times, take a bike ride, head to the beach, maybe even visit a bookstore. But far more than anything else he does, his vacation will be dominated by one thing: golf.

> This is where, each year, Obama gets the most concentrated amount of golf in. And he's now on pace to have a record year on the links.

His game was used to cultivate an elite crowd of powerbrokers around him, as the article went on to say:

> And he golfs like he governs. He goes with a small circle of friends and advisers (his Vineyard foursome almost always includes aide Marvin Nicholson and friend Eric Whitaker). He rarely engages with other politicians (one exception was a game with then-New York City Mayor Michael Bloomberg) but occasionally invites celebrities (last year comedian Larry David joined him).

Obama was a dedicated golfer and had installed a golfing simulator in the White House to improve his game. The optics of improvement and betterment was a subtle way to show it. He used golf as an allegory of his own tenure and the fortunes of the country. When he was criticized for his outings, the previous president came to his defense in 2013:

> Former President George W. Bush said President Obama should not be criticized over his frequent golf outings.

> Bush, who himself was criticized for his golfing as president, called the rounds "important for the president."

> "I see our president criticized for playing golf. I don't. I think he ought to play golf."

One of those critics would be the next president. Donald Trump is more than a controversial president; he is an enigmatic one. While he famously ridiculed

Obama for playing golf, Trump himself is considered to be a better golfer than the former reigning champ Kennedy and plays the sport almost as often as Eisenhower did. More interestingly, he owns nineteen golf clubs globally, making his association with the sport rival that of the Bush Dynasty. He has played his entire adult life, and has more than an interest in the game: he has business interests in it as well.

Yet throughout his public pre-White House life, golf was part of his package, as one April 8, 1984, *New York Times* article gushed:

> [Trump] talks boastfully about his projects, but is uncomfortable talking about himself. He does not smoke and does not drink alcohol. He plays golf and tennis regularly. His wife describes him as an all-American boy who likes country music best and prefers a steak and baked potato to anything called cuisine.

Yet by the time he became president, the gushing was clearly over, and his game was used as a symbol of something else, as the September 2, 2019 edition of *Time* magazine did:

> As Hurricane Dorian, one of the strongest Atlantic hurricanes on record, slammed through the Bahamas en route towards the Southeastern United States, President Donald Trump was spotted on the links at a Trump-branded Virginia golf club.
>
> The President has no plans listed on his public schedule for Monday. He was originally set to spend this weekend in Poland commemorating the start of World War II. However, that trip was canceled as the threat posed by Hurricane Dorian became more clear.
>
> Trump was also seen at the golf course on Saturday.

He played golf with then New England Patriots quarterback Tom Brady, which made headlines pre-presidency. Brady recounted his game with Trump to *GQ* magazine in an article that appeared on November 18, 2015:

> I asked him about playing golf with Donald Trump. He explained how this is an amazing experience, and how you never really know what the actual score is, and that there's always some sort of side bet, and that Trump always goes home with the money. I ask him if this means

Trump cheats, as it's hard to imagine how someone could always win, particularly since Golf Digest estimates Brady's handicap as an 8.

"Nah," says Brady. "He just—he doesn't lose. He just doesn't lose."

The golfing continued into the beginning of the presidency for some time after as NBC Sports recounted on January 25, 2017:

Tom Brady and President Donald Trump sound like fierce competitors on the golf course.

Corey Lewandowski, who managed the president's campaign, provided some insight into the relationship between Brady and Trump.

"Well, they're friends," Lewandowski told CSNNE's Gary Tanguay during 'Tanguay Takes America.' "They've had a long relationship, a long friendship. I know that the president respects Tom and his competitive nature, and how good he is, because Trump loves winners, and Tom's one of the greatest winners ever. But what I think the president also likes more than anything is that he can beat Tom at golf."

Tanguay had a hard time believing Trump can actually beat Brady.

"Oh, he does," Lewandowski said. "He's an excellent golfer."

Despite the symbol of triumph over even younger professional athletes, eventually, golf also became a symbol of his defiance, but also of his image. He played the sport with celebrities such as Kid Rock as *Newsweek* noted on March 22, 2022:

In an interview with *Fox News* that aired on Monday night, the 51-year-old musician confirmed he still plays golf with Trump and admitted it was a "little different" after the election but now Trump "seems great" and "sharp."

…"He just knows how to have fun," Rock said when explaining why he enjoys Trump's company on the golf course. "Doesn't take it too seriously. He's engaging. He's just cutting it up, open with politics."

Trump would upgrade a golfing simulator that had already been at the White House as the February 13, 2019 edition of *Time* noted:

President Trump has installed a room-sized golfing simulator inside his personal quarters at the White House, the Washington Post reported on Wednesday.

The device, which reportedly cost $50,000, will enable the President to simulate playing on some of the world's most famous golf courses. Trump paid for the simulator and its installation himself, according to the report.

The system replaced a less-sophisticated simulator that had been installed by President Barack Obama.

The competitiveness between presidents manifested itself in other ways, but it was a way to show his abilities were aligned with his numerous properties. It became a product placement of sorts, and a way to tweak his nose at the press who once discussed his abilities in glowing terms.

Each president had his own motives for taking up the sport, and each had their own strengths and weaknesses. For some, it had been a release. For others, to cultivate an inner circle. Still, others made alliances within their own government, while others saw it as an opportunity for global alliances. What becomes clear is that not a single swing was wasted, and the results of their game would shape history.

Chapter Four
Stories from the White and Green

A leader is a mythical figure. Most who vote for the leader have never met or interacted with the person in any capacity in a meaningful way. There is no expertise or experience in the leader for the average citizen, and yet, there must be trust. We need to feel secure enough with our choice at the polling station to give a complete stranger enormous power over our day-to-day lives.

It is the reason why people are always looking for details: the subtle signs that their choice is the best one. Who is this person? How do they think? What makes them tick?

It is the need to put a face on a story that drives much of journalism: to personalize and add color and personal anecdotes so that audiences can understand and relate to a person. The details, and the color of a person make it seem to their audience that they know the person. We can imagine a president in a suit sitting in the Oval Office. We can imagine the Commander in Chief boarding Air Force One. We can even imagine the leader at Davos or a G-8 Summit, but we cannot relate to it.

But sport is something different. It humanizes someone who is out of reach. When Eisenhower played, the *New York Times* covered it as an event in February 1953 with the headline: *Seen a Golfer on the White House Lawn? It's Eisenhower, Keeping His Eye on the Ball*. It was a newsworthy event with a personalized touch. It is a dream come true, and a sign of arrival.

Seeing presidents on their seeming "downtime" shows them out of their suits and stuffy atmosphere. It should be little wonder that the public and press alike have had a fascination with the sport of presidents: we see the human side of the leader and remember something other than someone speaking behind a dais.

A more personalized look at news coverage of presidents and their golfing habits shows us something about the leader: how they behave in a more mundane setting, even if the setting is anything but mundane. There could be a high-stakes meeting taking place, but to the untrained eye, it looks as if the leader is letting off a little steam. Lyndon Johnson pushed through the 1964 Civil Rights Act by re-negotiating with holdouts right on the links. Bill Clinton negotiated with the Canadian Prime Minister numerous times on the golf course in front of the full view of the news media without anyone knowing what was going on. The links were often an extension of the White House yet in a very subtle way.

Yet to the press, golf is a mirror to the president's character as he unwinds, and is often fair game for praise or criticism.

When the Commander in Chief is unpopular, it come often seen that the president spends too much time on the green, even if the president is conducting business with his sport. When people begin to sour, the assumption that the president is goofing off on the job, or being frivolous, even if the president is spending no more than what others have done.

The *Toronto Star* took umbrage with where Donald Trump played hardball with their native land of Canada in a September 2018 article:

> Facing demands from members of his own party to include Canada in any new North American trade deal, U.S. President Donald Trump threatened Saturday to keep Canada out- and to terminate the existing NAFTA if Congress tried to prevent him from proceeding with Mexico alone.
>
> …He issued the threat as he was driven to a Trump golf club in Virginia while a National Cathedral memorial service for the late Republican senator John McCain was underway.

But when President Clinton and "first golfer" was playing golf with the Prime Minister in April 1996, *Star* found it charming:

> Remember the Prime Minister who promised not to go fishing with the president of the United States?
>
> That would be Jean Chretien, who prefers to meet Bill Clinton on the golf course.

Chretien, who took great delight in mocking prime minister Brian Mulroney as president George Bush's fishing buddy, slipped into Washington unannounced last week and joined Clinton for 18 holes of golf Saturday at the Congressional Country Club.

It can also be seen as hijinks, as the *Hamilton Spectator* did in 1998 when it
referred to President George H.W. Bush's "speed golf" as "goofy golf." In February
1995, then-president Clinton golfed with two former Republican presidents —
Ford and Bush, with some shocking results as Reuters recounted:

"Fore!" yelled former President Ford as his first tee shot hooked left and
had gallery onlookers leaping for cover.

Former President Bush's second shot caromed off a tree into the crowd,
hitting spectator Norma Early. It smashed into the bridge of her nose,
breaking her glasses and causing heavy bleeding. Bush apologized and
commiserated with her as she was helped into a golf cart.

Sometimes even being president doesn't guarantee you will get to play where
and when you want. Barack Obama found out the hard way in September 2004,
according to NBC's Today show:

WILLIE GEIST: Matt, good morning. The President was just outside
New York City over Labor Day weekend to attend the wedding of his
former Chef Sam Cass and he hoped to sneak in a round of golf. But
when his advance team made request for the President to play a team,
several elite courses reportedly turned him away.

According to several …some of the New York area's top country clubs
including the Trump National Golf Club, Winged Foot, and Willow
Ridge turned down requests for President Obama to play around over
Labor Day weekend. Club managers saying they didn't want to incon-
venience their high-profile and dues-paying members by shutting down
their courses to accommodate the President during the busy holiday
weekend.

BRUCE BECK (WNBC Sports Anchor): It's probably the most important weekend of the year for golf, and two hundred and forty members are not going to say, hey, let the President come out, I'm not going to play this weekend. There's no way that would ever happen.

But it can also be seen as a sophisticated endeavor, so long as it does not seem as if the president is playing too much. President Taft was credited with making golf popular, but he was also seen as a victim of his own poshness. In a May 22, 1909 article in the *Spokane Press*, there was a headline that read, "Obsequious 'rubbernecks' sicken Taft of golf, the president was vexed by his own popularity on his seeming downtime":

Too much friendly curiosity on the part of the public threatens to end President Taft's golf playing.

"I had hoped," he said, "that I might play once or twice a week, but if a crowd attends every time I go to the links, I'll have to stop. There's no fun in going around the course with a lot of people at your heels."

The officials of the Chevy Chase Golf Club will do everything in their power to guard the president against outside interference, but as the links cover a great deal of ground, and are not surrounded by trespasser proof fences, it is impossible to prevent outsiders from trailing in behind the president.

The article then tried to soften the blow as it assured the American people that Taft wasn't some sort of jittery character:

The president is not of a nervous disposition, but naturally this gets on his nerves.

But the importance of the personal touch remains strong. St. Augustine Florida's World Golf Hall of Fame has in its collection, President Eisenhower's golf socks on display. He was also credited for making Rene Lacoste's alligator logo shirts popular golfing attire.

But to Eisenhower, it was not just about starting fashion trends. His famous association with golfing great Arnold Palmer is well-documented, and it was the president who encouraged Palmer to be a role model. Eisenhower took the game as a symbol of something more than mere intellectual or physical prowess.

The press saw the game differently and studied each president's ability even before the inauguration.

For example, *Time* magazine devoted an entire article *How Good is Barack Obama at Golf?* Looking at how well the President-elect was at the game, the piece had begun speculation even before the winner took the reins of power. The December 31, 2008, article went right down to business — and they were not exactly impressed with his game:

> President-elect Barack Obama's rise to the pinnacle of political power and his ability to enthrall giant crowds with his skills as an orator have drawn comparisons to former President John F. Kennedy. Those comparisons do not, however, carry over to the golf course.

The mediocre game-playing wasn't necessarily a foregone conclusion, however:

> Obama is clearly not as comfortable on the links as he is at the speaker's podium or the basketball court. Obama has played golf three times during his trip home to Hawaii for the Holidays, and each time he has looked less than presidential, but not terrible, according to local professionals. Norman-Ganin S. Asao, the head professional at Olomana Golf Links where Obama learned the game as a teenager and where he plays at least once during each trip home to Honolulu, says Obama has "maybe a 20'something handicap" based on the swings he's seen. "He's not a bad golfer at all," says Asao. "I've definitely seen a lot worse."

And he was already being assessed in relation to past presidents.

According to *Golf Digest*, Obama ranks eighth among the list of golfing Presidents, behind Bill Clinton but ahead of Ronald Reagan. Unlike JFK, who ranks number 1 on the Golf Digest list of 15, Obama does not shoot consistently in the 80's nor does not he play 100 rounds a year like Dwight Eisenhower (who is second on the list).

It becomes an easy method of determining presential capabilities, but for others, it can be an interesting measure in profound ways. The *Times of London* once published a Letter to the Editor from a prominent politician in 2003 who saw golf as having a more important role in political life:

From Mr. Stuart Bell, MP for Middlesbrough (Labour)

Sir, John F. Kennedy did indeed make fun of the spike marks in the Oval Office where former President Eisenhower used to practice his golf shots (leading article, July 11). However, I believe that one day the chiefs of staff came to see Eisenhower with a file marked Vietnam. They urged him to commit ground forces in order to prevent a communist takeover of the south.

Eisenhower measured his golf shot, shook his head, and, without taking his eye off the ball, said: "No. Once you get the troops in you'll never get them out."

He continued with his practice.

Kennedy committed thousands of American troops as observers and these became an army under Lyndon Johnson. Tens of thousands of American servicemen lost their lives in Vietnam, with thousands wounded.

Perhaps Kennedy, too, should have practiced some golf shots.

The sport of presidents is seen to be a mirror of the player's soul — and is seen by many as the game of reason: with each stroke, a leader has time to reflect on decisions that will impact billions of people and alter the course of history.

But golf is also fair game to use for political combat as the next chapter shows.

Chapter Five
In the Trenches

The importance of the sport in the highest office cannot be overstated: in over a century, the sport has become a symbol of cool strategy and long-term planning by a single leader. While some vestiges of the folksy notion that golf is a mere pastime are still employed from time to time, most presidents used their time on the links to broker deals, give an audience to policy-makers, and negotiate through various international quagmires.

Golf is so central to the myth of the presidency that it has become an issue in several presidential campaigns in both positive ways, and negative ones.

For example, the Scripps' owned *Chicago Day Book*, an advertising-free working-class newspaper, had Taft's golf-playing as a running gag. Some of the highlights of snark include:

- Everywhere, U. S. Teddy Wilson and Bryan draw big crowds. Taft plays golf.

- Taft played golf today. His language while playing is not recorded.

- Our own opinion is that as a president, Taft is a-fine golf player, and as a candidate, Roosevelt is fine annexer of campaign contributions, and that they both talk too much with their faces.

- Let us hope for Taft's sake there will be good golf weather on Nov. 6.

The press has often used golf to take cheap swings at presidents, and candidates have also done the same. The sport of presidents is fair game in personal attacks. As it is the symbol of both power and prowess, it can also be used as a symbol of overly leisure pursuits.

For Woodrow Wilson, the dig was deep in the July 7, 1912 edition of the *Daily Missoulian*:

Others fretted and fumed and stewed, but Woodrow Wilson, who had more occasion to be excited over the situation than any of the mere delegates, remained calm through it all. Wilson enjoys a game of golf as few men do, and people say they saw him frequently on the links while the democratic convention wrangled over whether it should give him the highest honor in its power to bestow or deliver the plum to some other candidate. Wilson got so interested in several of the games that he played during the convention that he apparently forgot that there ever was any such thing as a democratic party or a place known as the White House.

The game has repeatedly factored into several presidential campaigns, from Kennedy's to Trump's. It has been yielded as a weapon at times, and for others, there is the excitement that a golfer is about to become Commander in Chief. When Eisenhower was asked by one reporter during a press conference whether the president "procured helicopters" to go golfing in 1957, the president became irate as he angrily denied the accusation.

John F. Kennedy was one of the best golfers who made it to the White House, but it would have been hard to tell from his campaign which repeatedly derided Eisenhower's love of the sport. The *Times of London* had taken the optic divide into Kennedy's presidency, as they noted in a 1962 article:

> During the last administration, its leaders were constantly entertained at the White House, and in turn President Eisenhower shot over their magnificent estates and played golf at their private clubs. All this stopped when President Kennedy took over. The soft drinks barons and other notables were replaced on the invitation list by Nobel prize winners, artists, writers, and others with some knowledge of the French language and culture.

Kennedy had even let the Putting Green grow out as a symbolic gesture but eventually returned it to its former usability. He was also careful not to be seen playing the game during his presidency as he was aware of the optics of it. As the *New York Times* recounted:

> Some looked askance at Eisenhower's choice of companions. In 1959, Senator John F. Kennedy acidly told the historian Arthur M. Schlesinger Jr. that he would have expected Eisenhower, the World War II hero, to

be playing golf with his old army friends, but carped that "all his golfing pals are rich men he has met since 1945."

But Kennedy repeatedly kept his game under the radar as former *Washington Post* executive editor and presidential friend Ben Bradlee had recounted:

> But Kennedy is fun to play golf with, once you get out of sight of the sightseers, primarily because he doesn't take the game seriously and keeps up a running conversation. If he shanks one into the drink, he could let go with a broad-A "bahstard," but he would be teeing up his next shot instantly. With his opponent comfortably home in two and facing a tough approach, he might say "No profile needed here, just courage," a self-deprecating reference to his book, *Profiles in Courage.*

Kennedy's strategy would give him something in common with Donald Trump: Trump also repeatedly lambasted Obama's playing golf, though, unlike Kennedy, Trump has no qualms golfing in public as he shrugs off criticisms.

But Trump was not the only one to shrug them off. Obama did not back down through any of the golf shaming, as *Golf World* noted in October 2015:

> If Barack Obama was susceptible to golf shaming, it would have happened a long time ago. The president's frequent on-course excursions are often the subject of Republican ridicule. His most vocal critic these days, presidential candidate Donald Trump, released an Instagram video this summer that juxtaposed Obama laughing in a golf cart with ISIS propaganda footage. The subtext is that Obama should be spending less time working on his short game and more time rooting out terrorism. But from his earliest days in office, Obama has resisted the premise that it's an either-or proposition. According to an official count by CBS News' Mark Knoller, Obama has played 256 rounds while in office, far less than Woodrow Wilson (more than 1,000 rounds) or Dwight Eisenhower (more than 800) but still a healthy number in an era when a commander in chief's every move is chronicled in some form or another. And the president appears increasingly open about his unabashed love for the game.

The Obama-Trump golf feud narrative was a strong one, with the *Christian Science Monitor* wondering which man was the better golfer in 2015 (using the word versus in its headline), but within the same piece, the reporter noted:

> After President Barack Obama and former President Bill Clinton played golf together on Saturday, the topic of the game as a presidential attribute is making the rounds — and it turns out that GOP candidate Donald Trump's golfing prowess may giving him a political edge.

The article also noticed that for one exception (Ford and Carter), when a non-golfer runs for president against the golfer, the golfer is usually the one that wins the election. The piece also noted that "In the 2016 presidential race so far, the only candidate who is considered a "golfer" is Donald Trump."

Yet Obama used the golf course to conduct business as well, as the *Washington Post* recounted in February 2011:

> After months of public anticipation, President Obama and House Speaker John A. Boehner (R-Ohio) have settled on a date to play golf together: June 18.

Obama's and Boehner's offices confirmed the date Friday afternoon. No other details would be released about the golf match, according to the speaker's aides.

Boehner is widely considered the much better player, having started when he was in his 20s. Obama wasn't really a regular player until he became president. Of late, however, Obama has been improving his game, as Boehner's has deteriorated.

The "golf summit" as it was dubbed by the press, took place in June of that year — with good publicity, but a lack of concrete political breakthroughs, according to the *Post*:

> The golf summit on Saturday may not have resolved the partisan argument over the deficit and the debt ceiling or the legality of the U.S. military operation in Libya. But some good came of it, at least for the victors. The bipartisan pairing of President Obama and House Speaker John A. Boehner (R-Ohio) won the 18th hole and the match against Vice President Biden, thought to be the strongest player in the group, and Ohio Gov. John Kasich (R). To the winners go the spoils, in this case $2 each.

It would not be the last time Obama used golf for both political persuasion and good publicity as the August 2015 *Washington Post* reported:

> But two weekends ago, for the first time during his presidency, Obama played a round of golf with rank-and-file House Democrats at the Courses at Joint Base Andrews in Maryland.

Although all of the participants said the event was entirely social, the overture served as the latest demonstration that, in his seventh year in the White House, Obama is using the tools of personal persuasion more often than before in his presidency.

For Obama golf was a powerful tool to keep his party unified as he projected an image to the public, showing that he was not bowing to Trump's criticisms.

Speaking of Trump's campaign, his former New York golf course caddy and general manager of Trump National Golf Club Westchester Daniel Scavino was recruited to be his social media director. Scavino generated controversy when he posted an image that seemed to many as being anti-Semitic. Trump cheekily launched his campaign by inviting Obama to play golf at his one of his own courses. The president declined.

Trump's golfing was also used against him by former presidential rival Ted Cruz who had accused the president of being former House Speaker John A. Boehner's "texting and golfing buddy." Both the *New Yorker* and *The Economist* also used his love of the game as criticism, with the *New Yorker's* cover a cartoon of Trump breaking the windows of the White House with his swing.

Yet when he was elected, Trump could be seen on the links frequently, and as he owns many courses across the globe, it seemed like an odd criticism to make of the previous president, particularly as he all but launched his presidential bid on his own golf course, yet the incongruence remains.

And has been used as fodder from political rivals, such as Democratic hopeful Mike Bloomberg in February 2020 when he paid for billboards that proclaimed in red letters that Trump "cheats at golf."

The image of a golfing president is not a monolithic one: sometimes it is revered; other times, it is an attack, yet in all of the bluster, it is rarely a sport a former president leaves behind. When Trump was playing a public golf game on his New Jersey course two years after leaving office, *Newsweek* noted one conservative media host who praised the former president on July 30, 2022: "These kinds of things you can't really quantify, who do you want to have a beer with? Who would you rather hang out with? Who do you have more trust and who looks more powerful in a position," though his hosting a Saudi-backed LIV Golf tournament at his course was not without controversy. Most presidents continue to play long after their term is over, as their love of the game is genuine as it is linked to their way of strategizing, and it is the way they focus themselves as they brokered deals, commanded attention, took risks, made alliances, overcame obstacles, and won the highest office in the nation.

Chapter Six
The Early Days

Golf was not part of the presidential package until President William H. Taft was its pioneer. It is a peculiar contribution to make to the mystique of the game, but it would be one of the most important contributions to the Office. Twenty-six presidents before him did not golf, but after his tenure, it would become standard, with the last seven presidents in office all being golfers, regardless of political leaning or background. It was too big and flexible of a symbol to abandon.

But Presidents Taft, Wilson, and Harding are the defining pioneers of the link between the president and the sport of golf, and it is interesting to observe how each man-made use of the game during their time in office.

To that extent, it is simpler to see the basic scaffolding for each pioneer in order to see their overall strategy: Taft used golf to inspire, Wilson to persevere, and Harding to express competent panache.

Taft's genuine love of the game helped anchor the sport into the Presidential Mythos: his exuberance was contagious. He looked like he was having *fun*. His images out on the green were always dynamic and energetic. He looked *happy*, and the game became him.

Moreover, his golfing entourage was enviable: when a who's who of industry titans and powerbrokers came along for the ride, suddenly, this was no longer a game: this was part and parcel of the American Dream.

Taft established golf and a prestigious company as part of the presidency even before he formally took office. The November 7, 1908 edition of the *Evening Statesman* made this link clear to the American people:

> Senator Jonathan Bourne has gone to Hot Springs to play golf with President-Elect Taft. The series of games which Taft and Bourne were playing some time ago were interrupted by the campaign, but when Taft and the senator appeared it was agreed between them that they should

meet again at Hot Springs, November 10 and continue the amusement. Senator Bourne left for Hot Springs yesterday, and will not return to Portland until after congress adjourns. He will spend about two weeks at the resort and will then go on to Washington.

It is an interesting wrinkle that no less than a *presidential campaign* got in the way of their golf game, but not for long. It is all about winning, and alliances as the article went on to note:

Their mutual fondness for the guttapercha ball is a bond of common interest between Bourne and the president-elect which makes it probable that the Oregon senator will rank even higher in the counsels of the next administration than he has in those of Roosevelt's regime. as he was never a member of the tennis cabinet: and in the new golf cabinet he should surely rank high.

During his tenure, there would be *hundreds* of newspaper articles devoted in whole or in part to his love of the game. The of the *Evening Star* under a section entitled *Taft Plays Golf*:

Judge Taft was today entirely free from politics so far as conferences were concerned. A game of golf in the morning and a drive with Gen. Henry C. Corbin in the afternoon were the day's plans for recuperation and exercise.

Even on the day of his inauguration, the press made a point of bringing up his great passion, as the *Coeur D'Alene Evening Press* did on March 4, 1909:

President Taft is deliberate; Ex-President Roosevelt is impulsive. President Taft exercises at golf to keep down his weight; Ex-President Roosevelt rides, runs, shoots, boxes, wrestles, fences, or plays tennis to down the other fellow, or for the love of the sport itself. President Taft was graduated at Yale; Ex-President Roosevelt halls from Harvard. President Taft tips the beam at 300 pounds; Ex-President Roosevelt weighs 100 less.

This established theme would remain consistent throughout Taft's presidency: golf was part of his *essence*. Some, such as previous President Theodore Roosevelt thought Taft was too avid a golf player and advised him to hang up his clubs —

to no avail, of course. He was methodical and sociable: his game reflected this nexus and sent a distinct message because of it. Having friends in high places meant the green was his secondary *office*. In a March 28, 1909 article in the *Washington Sunday Star,* the vintage narrative was fully in play:

> William Howard Taft played yesterday afternoon his first game of golf since he entered the White House as President of the United States. For nearly three hours he trudged the links at Chevy Chase, playing a four-ball match with Vice President Sherman as a partner against Gen. Clarence Edwards and Capt. Archibald W. Butt. The cards were not turned in at the end of the game, and consequently, the score is not known.

The point was not about winning a game, but getting down to business. The article paraded more names to build an impressive scaffolding:

> The full eighteen holes were not played, because a high wind, accompanied by a nasty rain, drove the players to the clubhouse with three holes left unplayed. In addition to the President and Vice President. Secretary Knox was on the links. He played eighteen holes against Huntington Wilson.

Other details about the security detail were also mentioned:

> The President's party went to the club in an automobile, arriving there at 3 o'clock. Two secret service men accompanied the automobile, following it on motorcycles. They did not appear on the course, except to walk around part of it with "Jimmy" Douglass, the club professional.

Who was on the green with the Commander in Chief would be common fodder in stories of this kind:

> The President did not waste much time in getting into his golfing clothes, and he appeared to be very much pleased when he scanned the fair greens and saw that they were in good condition and that there were many players out. The first thing he did after leaving the clubhouse was to ask for his friend, W. J. Boardman. Mr. Boardman was playing a round with Benjamin Miller, and spied Mr. Taft from the middle of the second green. He waved his hand to the President, and the President waved his hat in recognition.

The Vice President would also be a common fixture in these vignettes:

Vice President Sherman was the last man of the party to make his appearance on the links. He wore flannel trousers and a cardigan jacket — a sleeveless affair, which showed a heavy gray shirt. As he walked to the tee Mr. Taft said: "Doesn't Mr. Sherman remind you of one of those sporty Englishmen?" Mr. Sherman had anticipated the game, as he was on the links for a bit of practice Friday.

When it came to golf, there was no detail too small for the press, but the deeper psychological signs were just as important. Insights into the man could be gleaned from his method of golfing. For example, in the April 13, 1909 edition of the *Evening Times-Republican*, an article *Taft as a Golfer* had spent a good deal of time showing readers how the game was a window into the man they elected to lead them:

Of course, the real reason President William H. Taft plays golf is because it's golf, and, if you don't believe that just arrange to have a little talk with him after he has played a good winning game and then try one after he has lost. Mention golf casually and see what happens. You will always have the Taft sunshine, for that is never dimmed, but if things have gone wrong on the links you will catch a shadow or two between smiles.

This first-hand account was a fascinating insider's account:

I recall one evening in the Taft cottage at Hot Springs, Va. Mr. Taft was stretched out in a comfortable armchair before a big log fire. He had just come in from his worst game on the Hot Springs course and was still in his golf clothes. He looked solemnly at himself for a few seconds, then at the blaze.

"Well," said he finally, "I've played golf for ten years or more, and I know at last that I'm a dub-a-dub, pure and simple."

The plaint was none the less genuine if it did run into a hearty laugh.

The vignettes would continue to paint a fuller picture of the man:

On the other hand, there was an occasion at Augusta when it would have been cruel even to have suggested the memory of this Hot Springs confession. That was when Mr. Taft did the course in eighty-eight making a new record for himself.

The news of his feat preceded him, and as he left the golf grounds several of his friends stepped up to congratulate him.

"Back, back; don't touch me!" said he, with mock superiority. Then be smiled his broadest and confessed that it was his happiest day in Augusta. That night before 200 members of the Augusta chamber of commerce he admitted be bad a "swelled bead" over the score, adding in a spirit of fun that he didn't know whether he would rather have made that record or been elected president of the United States.

With golf, a single blunt self-assessment would spark an immediate trend:

Under ordinary circumstances, though, Mr. Taft Is a very modest golfer. He would rather surprise than disappoint his friends. He is the first man who has ever been brave enough to admit that he plays golf "bumblepuppy." He was speaking of a talk he had had with Jerome D. Travers, the amateur.

"We talked," said Mr. Taft "of such things as would suggest themselves to an expert and a man who plays bumblepuppy."

The next day all the newspapers had footnotes explaining what bumblepuppy is. Now the word goes prancing over the links in company with "mollycoddle," and every golfer has come to admit that at one time or other he belonged to the "bumble" breed of canines.

But the final assessment would heap high praise on the Commander in Chief:

A walk around the golf links with Mr. Taft is a tonic. He golfs in the same way that he does everything else—with patience and the best of nature. He lets his opponents sputter and explode, but plods on himself from the first green to the last with never a break in temper and with a Taft laugh always on tap.

It is easy to see why the allure of golf would inspire other presidents to take up the game. The potential for good press and subtextual messages was too great to resist.

And the press understood the potential, too. The *Detroit Times* certainly understood the importance: in a July 19, 1915 article entitled *Golf Sport of Presidents — Taft Popularizes Game*, noted his contribution a mere *two years* after he left Office:

> One of these days someone will write of the sport and recreations of our presidents. Their various biographers are silent in most instances, whether from a lack of information or because most of our rulers were not athletically inclined, it is a moot point.
>
> In fact, there are only four that were genuine sportsmen, as we know the term.
>
> …Taft and Wilson are not only baseball fans, but golfers as well. The former was the chief executive who made golf popular with thousands of Americans who hitherto showed little or no interest in the game which now claims a half million enthusiastic devotees in this country. As a golfer there seems little doubt that he is the superior of his successor, although the two have never played together.

Taft's enthusiasm sparked a trend with the people, and it is no surprise that golf became ingrained in the U.S. thanks to the president who had an upbeat disposition. To lead an electorate and quietly push them out in the open as they became inspired to live life as their leader was breathtaking. It only took *one* president to create the part of the mythos, and it was the *first* who made it happen as it sparked a craze and found a subtle, but effective way to maintain some control of his own narrative. It would be a hard, but not impossible, act to follow.

So influential was Taft's love of the game that it began to make a cultural shift according to the *Los Angeles Herald* on June 20, 1909:

> Golf threatens to rival baseball as a popular game on account of President Taft's devotion to the links. So far, the president has not found many people to play with, but a golf cabinet will doubtless be organized in due time to replace…Roosevelt's famous tennis cabinet. Tennis is admittedly a back number now in official circles in Washington, even the presidential tennis court, which was the scene of many historic encounters during the Roosevelt administration, is to be destroyed and used as

the site for a new wing of the executive office bulling…Taft is the pioneer golfing president…

President Woodrow Wilson, on the other hand, did not generate the same
quantity of headlines as did Taft when it came to golf, though he was a dedicated
player who would golf before breakfast, and was known to hit red-colored balls in
the snow. There were many reasons, but Taft was a hard act to follow. However,
Wilson's golf-playing was established in the press while he was governor of New
Jersey. An interesting example was noted in the June 26, 1912 edition of the *Cairo
Bulletin:*

> Gov. Woodrow Wilson was playing golf here when word reached him
> this afternoon of the selection of Judge Parker ae temporary chairman
> of the Democratic national convention. He declined to discuss the result
> of the polling with newspaper men.

The groundwork was already set: there is no time for rest for the governor: even
his golf game would be interrupted by important events. He is on-call and has to
take snatches of breaks whenever he can.

Once he became president, any biographical tidbits from the press almost always mentioned his golf-playing prominently. It was the way to know him. The
Riverside Daily Press had done so on December 28, 1915:

> President Wilson celebrated his 59th birthday today quietly with his
> bride. The only indication that the executive has passed another mile-
> stone was the scores of telegrams from his friends in all parts of the
> world. In health and spirit the president is many years younger than 59.
> His hair is quite gray, but he stands erect. 5 feet 11 inches in his stocking
> feet. Recently he tipped the scales at 171 pounds. He walks a great deal
> and plays lots of golf. Woodrow Wilson was born at Staunton, Va., De-
> cember 28, 1856. His father was the Rev. Joseph R. Wilson, a distin-
> guished scholar and clergyman of the south, and his mother, Jes-
> sie Woodrow Wilson. His ancestry on both sides is Scotch-Irish.

Just like Taft, those who knew Wilson from golfing circles could count on
significant press coverage: while the golf course was already an extension of the
White House, it was seen as the place where the *real* president could unwind and
take off the mask. However, the inner circle was a sign that someone had *arrived,*

even after the president left office. Such was the case in one *Colusa Herald* profile on December 4, 1924:

> Donald Ball, golf instructor for millionaires and friend of President Woodrow Wilson, is in Colusa. Just now Ball is giving golf lessons at the Colusa Country club.

> Ball is an Englishman and he knows golf. At various times he has been professional at the Washington Golf club, which was the first club at Washington, D. C., the Columbia Golf club, the Newport Golf club and the Narragansett Pier Country club where he has met people of all nationalities, congressmen, presidents and just plain people.

Golf was a prime newspeg, and the article and there would be no higher newsmaker than a president — even over the nation's wealthiest players:

> It wasn't the Goulds and the Astors and the Vanderbilts who interested Ball most, however, it was Wilson; not Wilson the president, or Wilson the college professor, but just the plain, quiet Woodrow Wilson who made his rounds on the golf links three or four times a week.

> "He was a great chap," Ball said, smiling as he recalled the president's visits to the course where he was professional before the war. War cares hadn't made their mark on the man who became the world's leading statesman. "Wilson was just a good fellow when he came on the links," Ball continued. "He forgot all about his office duties and just came out to enjoy himself. He and his friend and physician, Dr. Grayson, always came together and they had some hot games, I'll tell you. Both of them shot the course somewhere around 90."

Wilson was known to golf with his personal physician in Virginia to unwind, hinting at a more therapeutic reason to partake in the game. Golf was seen as a gateway into a president's soul: not just his intellectual abilities and strategies: but who he was on his off-hours:

> Ball stopped for a moment to puff at his pipe. Then he went on: "Three secret service men always came out to the grounds with the president. One of them rode in the car with the president and two rode in

another machine which followed. The one man would follow the president…while the other two would stay at the clubhouse."

"There was nothing snobbish about Wilson," Ball declared after another short session with the pipe. "He was just the same as you or I. He was always jolly. When he sliced his ball into the rough, he took it all as a part of the game and never complained. He always would ask where his friend, Donald, was if he didn't see me when he started out. That's the kind of a man he was. If he'd see me giving a lesson down the course…

It was golf that let the American people know who was minding their nation's business, and the article concluded with an interesting anecdote of trust and chivalry that linked the golf course straight to the White House:

Ball has a letter from President Wilson thanking him for a gift of a golf club. Ball gave a club to the … "It was a funny thing," Ball asserted, "when I sent a fellow down to the White House with the clubs. He thought he wouldn't be able to go into the White House yard. He did, though. Those golf clubs and a little note I wrote did the trick. The president had a whole room full of clubs and balls, too. That's one advantage of being president. The golf manufactures have a good habit of sending the White House samples of new clubs." Ball values the letter from Wilson very highly. "It's a letter from a real fellow," Ball says.

There could no longer be any doubt that a president who golfed had an enormous advantage in the press, especially if he showed a softer and gentler side as much as showed a competitive streak. For instance, according to author Frank Cormier, the president's golfing may have saved a woman's life:

Woodrow Wilson, on a trip to Pass Christian, Texas, was returning from the golf course when he spotted smoke coming from the roof of a house. Rushing into the dwelling, he was greeted by a woman who, on recognizing him, invited the President into the parlor for a chat. "I haven't time to sit down," said Wilson. "Your house is on fire." The President and his party then formed a bucket brigade and extinguished the blaze. Wilson subsequently was elected to the Pass Christian Fire Department.

Golf was a singular balancing act: a president had to show emotional *literacy*. He was not just ambitious but understood something beyond pushing the country onto center stage. The game of golf suddenly became the most effective way to do it.

So important was the sportsmanship that ability took a backseat: it was up to the professional golfers to dazzle with their prowess, but presidents had to show that they did not fear playing a game in public or shy away just because they weren't the best on the field. Wilson showed he was willing to persevere, and this facet generated much intriguing praise for the man.

Nowhere was this delicate balance more succinctly presented than in the March 21, 1916 edition of the *San Luis Obispo Daily Telegram* under the seemingly unflattering headline, *CALLS PRESIDENT A "POOR GOLFER"; "KNOCKS BALL ABOUT", SAYS EXPERT*:

> If it were not for the fact that he is president, Woodrow Wilson might be classed as a "duffer" among golfers according to George Sargent, new professional at the Interlachen Club

But despite the ability, Wilson did not shy away from the sport:

> Sargent, for five years instructor to the nation's chief executives, William Taft and Wilson, on the links at Chevy Chase, Washington, says Wilson is an enthusiastic golfer but his game consists mostly of knocking the little sphere about.

Before international diplomatic relations became complicated, Wilson spent much time on the links. Sargent often accompanied the president and instructed him. Now the president does not get much time for golf. However, he manages to run out to the course of the Washington Suburban club, a short automobile ride from the executive mansion. This is a nine-hole course, and the president and Mrs. Wilson come out there, play one round and be back in an hour.

It was also noted in the piece that Taft was a hard act to follow when it came to the sport:

> Taft, when president, was a member of the Chevy Chase club, and played all his games there.

> Sargent opposed the former president in many matches and declares he is really a good player. Presidents of the United States are not the only high officials whom Sargent has taught.

But while Wilson's abilities didn't impress, his enthusiasm for the game would be a part of the legacy. For instance, the *Coronado Journal* on July 13, 1932, in an article entitled *Why Pres. Wilson was a Golf Duffer* had this tidbit to relay to readers:

> A new story about Woodrow Wilson has just come from Joe Horgan, golf caddy who used to carry the President's clubs at Deal Beach, New Jersey. "The President wasn't a good golfer," Morgan relates, "but he seemed to enjoy the game thoroughly. He laughed and joked a lot, and once, when he almost missed a shot completely, he blamed it on the fact that when he first took up golf, he had to play without a caddy for the sake of economy. He said that was when he learned to lift his head with each shot, a fatal habit for golfers.

Wilson was a war president: having to navigate through the Great War, and the press coverage of his golf game quietly allowed him to symbolically *speak* to the people: things in the world were not predictable, and there wasn't an easy solution, but his idealism and determination would guide them to better places. It should be no surprise that Wilson was in the middle of the game he was informed that a German U-boat had torpedoed the Lusitania. Germany was resuming its submarine campaign, but the image of a president having to deal with the most serious news even in a moment of respite was a powerful one.

Wilson's lack of talent for the game paralleled the chaos of war. He was out in open spaces on a different kind of field, but he wasn't going to back away: he would keep at it until the game was over. His decency out on the green came back to the citizens and set a rhythm to the game and a message: that even in chaos, there would be light and he would be the one to generate it.

Warren G. Harding cemented golf as something more than a presidential pastime: but a way to gain tangible accolades. Headlines blared about his recognition. For instance, *Harding Honored as One of "Leading Spirits of Golf"* was the headline in the *Morning Press* on January 15, 1922:

> President Warren G. Harding, declared to be one "of the leading spirits of golf tonight was named an honorary member of the United States Golf Association at its annual meeting...

Harding would see a boost in his profile thanks to his golfing manners and abilities, such as he did in the *San Francisco Call and Post* with the loud headline,

"WITH HARDING ON THE LINKS/DRAWS A BIG GALLERY/NATION'S GREATEST ATTRACTION" on August 8, 1921:

> Warren Gamaliel Harding is the nation's greatest golf attraction.

> "Chick" Evans, "Jock" Hutchison and "Bobby" Jones notwithstanding, Warren G. Harding has bigger gallery each time that he plays golf than any other golfer in the United States. If the President saw fit to charge "two bits" per for each person in his gallery every time he wields "brassie" he would net a neat little sum that might run a close second to the salary check that the Treasury Department sends him twice a month.

Harding seemed to be a *rock star* before his time, according to the piece:

> All Washington likes to watch the President golf, and to date most of Washington has seen him at the game. No one has heard him, which speaks well for his temper. The President plays most frequently on the nine hole course in East Potomac Park, which is maintained by the government for the public of Washington.

The aura of a deific leader who could command respect and attention absolutely anywhere was the kind of press most world leaders would envy:

> Whenever he appears at first tee, he is immediately surrounded by half hundred golfers and all of the way down the course has an increasing "gallery." Most of the golfers let the President "go through." while they stand on the edge of the fairway and watch him...

And once again, a president's golfing temperament played a significant part in the profile:

> Warren G. Harding's collective golf cards may not look well enough to be framed, but he is rare golfer, for he never displays extreme joy or chagrin over his game. Like most of the garden variety of golfers, he spends a good bit of his time in the bunkers and raises much dust. but. unlike most golfers, he doesn't raise "Cain" with the dust. He just shoots away until he is out of the hazard and back on the fairway...

Harding also saw the value of bringing in the press on his golf games in a significant way, cultivating the mystique. The *San Francisco Call* mentioned one such event on May 27, 1922:

Warren G. Harding of the Marion Star battled on the golf links yesterday with his colleagues of the Washington newspaper corps and won
4th prize, a box of gilt balls, in the annual tournament of the Washington Newspaper Golf Club.

The President rolled in a gross score of 91, equaling that of Lowell Mellett of
the Washington News, who won first place. But the Marion correspondent's handicap of 22 was two short of the tournament winner, who took the silver cup given
by Edward B. McLean, publisher of the Washington Post. While the tournament
was on, capital news was stymied. The President played with the local correspondents. newspaper owners, cartoonists, and others of the fourth estate.

The event was a coup in many regards. Harding took presidential golf to a new
level. It was an expedient way to deal with the press, reach out to the public, and
cultivate ties with various elites. Fascinatingly, newspapers would place Harding's
golfing outing above the cutline before mentioning his presidential itinerary.
Somehow, golf came *first*. The *Cordoba Daily Times* gave more prominence to
Harding's golf game than to his impending visit to Alaska on March 10, 1922:

> Immediately upon reaching his hotel yesterday afternoon, on his vaca-
> tion, President Warren G. Harding donned his golf clothes and, accom-
> panied by Speaker Gillette of the House of Representatives, Under Sec-
> retary of State Fletcher, and E. B. McLean, the Washington publisher,
> played eighteen holes on the St. Augustine links. Today the President
> planned to board Mr. McLean's palatial houseboat for a leisurely cruise
> down the coast, stopping only where golf can be played to advantage.
> Mr. Harding is said to be an excellent player.

But then came inspiration: if golf was the way to keep the lines flowing between
politicians and titans of industry inside the US, then it stood to reason it could be
used beyond the borders. Presidential golf allowed a new kind of quiet diplomacy.
Such a case was noted in the *San Pedro News Pilot* on June 28, 1923, under the
headline *Harding to Meet British Columbia Official on Links*:

> President Warren G. Harding's challenge to a tilt on the golf links of
> Vancouver, British Columbia, has been accepted by Lieut. Gov. W. C.
> Nichol. The match probably will be played on Harding's way back from
> Alaska.

In fact, Harding made news when he *didn't* golf, as one article in the *Evening Star* noted on November 24, 1920, when he was mere President-elect:

> Senator Warren G. Harding, United States President-elect, gave up golf and mooring this morning to make a personal study of the practical working of the Panama Canal. He planned to leave here at 8:30 o'clock on a government mine sweeper and looked forward to a leisurely Journey through the waterway.

Like Taft and Wilson, Harding's love of golf was well-established pre-presidency. With all three pioneering presidents creating an intricate weave of the sport, a new method to speak to the public was created and cultivated. Taft set the enduring trend and Wilson took up the mantle despite his lack of organic talent, while Harding parlayed his talent to awards and began to use the sport beyond the U.S. borders; thus, the Sport of Presidents began to flourish within the span of less than two decades. Each president contributed to a different, yet enduring facet of the game, but its trajectory and use would go into different and unexpected directions as the following chapter explains.

Chapter Seven
A Sport Comes Into Its Own

As we have seen, golf seemed to be the perfect secondary vehicle for a president to communicate different messages to different groups. The trinity of pioneers — Taft, Wilson, and Harding played the game flawlessly in that regard. They proved deft at using the game to cultivate an image, build bridges, and find an elegant way of bringing the public in to their off-hours. The images would always be pensive and dynamic, and it allowed the press to provide positive psychological insight into their leaders. This gave something else to the public: a safe and non-offensive way to talk politics at a cocktail party. Golf was the buffer to show someone took care to read a newspaper to keep up with current events, but in such a way as not to start arguments over the appetizers.

It allowed for something else: to bring civilized dialogue across party lines among the middle class: it would be acceptable for a political detractor to subversively question a president's golfing ability, while the supporter could counter about a president's stamina and willingness to play regardless of ability. Both sides could air their beliefs without coming to blows. The golf course became a neutral zone and a conversational safe haven.

The tradition would still continue with Presidents Calvin Coolidge, and Franklin D. Roosevelt who may have not picked up the clubs while in office, but still had their place. Each man had a very different relationship and use for the sport, but that both used the Sport of Presidents during their respective tenures to help foster the game and progress it in important and clever ways. Both understood the importance of linking golf to the highest office in the nation and ensured that they did. We will look at each one in turn.

This would be an era of quiet strategic pivots: Coolidge despised golf, and yet he was still *linked* to the game, while Roosevelt made the game more accessible. It was as if the Sport of Presidents had a life of its own and was growing up right in the White House. It is interesting to note that there was unspoken *pressure* on Coolidge as he ascended the presidency after Harding's death. The Quiet President, despite his disdain for the sport, kept the *spirit* of the game going nonetheless.

It is a huge stretch to consider Coolidge a golfer, and yet when he was Vice President under golf superfan Harding (who used the South Lawn as a golf range, having his dog Laddie Boy retrieve his drives), he could be seen at a golf course, but not as a player as the *Washington Herald* noted on July 22, 1921: "Vice President Calvin Coolidge attended the golf tournament at Columbia Country Club yesterday morning."

Interestingly enough, even when he was governor of Massachusetts, his non-golfing ways made news, as it did in the *Stockton Independent* on July 20, 1920:

> By way of adding to his hearty appetite for the splendid country rooking prepared by his father's housekeeper, the governor frequently goes into the meadows before the mist has cleared and mows a good-sized corner of the field before the I breakfast bell rings. He says it Is much more invigorating than golf and fully as remunerative although he humorously adds that "some chips make more at golf than they would at farming."

Coolidge made no secret that he preferred horseback riding to golf, and yet, the specter of golf was always hovering around him. The *Riverside Daily Press* also brought up his views on golf on July 9, 1920:

> "Silent Cal" is a name they have for Governor Calvin Coolidge in Hampshire county, Mass. "Smokes stogies, hates golf, likes hot biscuits and maple syrup," comments one New England writer describing the Republican nominee for vice president, "One of the canniest, cleverest, most epigrammatic speakers that ever slowly but surely climbed the political ladder," says another, adding that "Silent Cal" is a thorough master of English and the devoted husband of a vivacious wife whom he is said to have won with fewer words than ever before on record. They have two fine, manly boys, John, aged 12, and Calvin, Jr., 13. Governor Coolidge is accounted a hard worker. He is at his desk in the slate house every day from 9 to 5. Then he takes a walk for exercise. He won't

play golf of which game Senator Harding is very fond, because to the governor it merely seems to be knocking a little ball around a lot.

Yet Coolidge had golf clubs during his tenure as president (which he left behind when he left office), but his aversion to the sport was seen as *problematic*, and thus, had an unfortunate *flaw*. As the *San Bernardino Sun* fretted in a June 27, 1925 article headlined *"New England Papers Urge Coolidge Be Permitted to Have Vacation/PERSONALITY UNCHANGED/How He Will Spend Time Is Problem Friends Have Not Yet Solved"*:

> But what will Mr. Coolidge's recreation be? About the only thing he has done in the past has been to take trips on the Mayflower. He plays no golf or other games. It is suspected by his intimates that he doesn't know how to take a vacation.

Golf would not need Coolidge to endure in the White House in the long term, but according to the press and public consensus, Coolidge was in desperate need of golf. The first absence of a golfing president was met with disapproval, but without vitriol or disrespect.

However, there would be a gap as the 31st president Herbert Hoover was not a golfer, either; however, this trend would not continue.

Interestingly with Hoover, while he didn't play golf (as the *San Pedro News Pilot* declared in 1928, "Herbert Hoover doesn't dance, play golf or join in stag parties, but he likes fishing and motoring"); the press felt the need to find *someone* in his sphere who did. The same newspaper had an article about one such man — a Russian by the name of Kosta Boris on July 21, 1931:

> If a state function is in progress at the White House, Boris may be observed standing behind a column discreetly watching what is taking place. He lives at the White House in a room on the lop floor. He drives his own small car to one of the Washington parks frequently for a round of golf.

> When the President's grandchildren — Peggy Ann and Herbert III — were staying at the executive mansion, Boris acted as their guardian. With the two children, he was a great favorite. It was a familiar sight to see them in his care around the White House, and to hear them address Boris us "Uncle Charlie." Modest, at all times discreet, no word can be

drawn from him about his duties as valet to the President. To Boris those are things not to be discussed.

To the incessant kidding to which he is subjected by newspapermen, who cover the White House and accompany the President everywhere, Boris pays little heed. Sometimes he gets a bit serious, but is quick to sense when he is being joked. He is said to be a general favorite in the Hoover household.

Golf was equated with trustworthiness — and if the president didn't golf, at least his trusted foreign workers did, and it was still seen as a sign of honor.

The presidential golfing lull would break with the presidency of Roosevelt, but not in the way it had been in play previously.

Roosevelt was an avid golfer in his prime, though it was a serendipitous discovery for him. It was 1894 in Campobello, New Brunswick, Canada when the fog thwarted his plans to go sailing. It would be a fateful stroke of luck, and he continued. FDR frequently played golf before his presidency, mostly with other elites, such as politicians, including future president Taft. He was a golfer during his college days onwards, but the ravages of polio ended his golfing days before he was forty; however, he was determined that if he could not partake in golf, he could make it accessible to the public instead.

This would be a gift to the American people: federal funding would create 350 public golf courses, and create a link between the Sport of Presidents and those citizens who did not have the means to join clubs. Many survived throughout the decades, with the FDR Golf Club in Philadelphia surviving until 2019, though the Roosevelt Memorial Golf Course in Warm Springs, Georgia remains in play.

That it was during the Second World War that the game was given a presidential blessing to play did not go unnoticed in the *Globe and Mail* on April 16, 1942, under the headline *Golf is Given Wartime Go-Ahead by Roosevelt*:

Golf's greats got together here today for the Master's Golf Tournament — and got a double helping of cheerful news to start them off.

First was an announcement by Ed Dudley, head of the Professional Golfers Association that President Roosevelt had given golf a wartime go-ahead, along with baseball and other preparational pastimes of the United States.

…Dudley made public a letter from Stephen T. Early, secretary to President Roosevelt, transmitting to him the President's opinion that, within reasonable limits, he believed the war effort would not be hampered, but actually improved by sensible participation in healthful pursuits.

This decision eventually paved the way to bring the sport to wider acceptance: after all, the stresses of war were given an outlet worthy of a president. H.W. Brands noted in his book *Traitor to His Class: The Privileged Life and Radical Presidency of Franklin Delano Roosevelt*:

He loved playing golf more than just about anything else. I believe that his inability to play made the game even more important to him, and he liked the idea that government could make it possible for ordinary people to play.

It was a gift of paying it forward, and it created a stage that transferred the Sport of Presidents to all Americans, and a single sport showed how a president could pass his passion to the public: he may have been denied, but there was no reason for others to be denied as well. While this was the quiet era of presidential golf, it merely took a quiet transmutation before roaring back to life. After all, these were the war years, and FDR's inability to golf paralleled the zeitgeist of the era. Somehow, this absence was entirely fitting of the times.

There would be one more presidential skip with Harry S. Truman, but then there would be a president who would be *the* president most associated with the sport. After two quiet golfing presidents, it should be no surprise that there would be one who'd be more unleashed than the others — and that honor goes to Dwight D. Eisenhower.

Chapter Eight
The Golf President

When most observers think about *The Sport of Presidents*, it is President Dwight D. Eisenhower who stands out the most, even from pioneer Taft or enthusiast Harding. His reverence for the game was so great, that the U.S. Golf Association had, according to author George Sullivan, "installed a putting green outside the Oval Office" in 1954, complete with a sand trap, two holes, and with shrubbery to allow for the president to play with privacy. He was not the first president to golf, but he was the biggest fan of the sport and had a reverence for it, though sometimes his unrepentant love for the game did not always work in his favor.

For instance, on May 1, 1960, the Soviet Union had detected a U.S. Lockheed U-2 plane conducting secret recognizance missions and shooting it down, though the CIA pilot Francis Gary Powers survived and was captured by the Soviets. Then leader Nikita Khrushchev became so incensed during the back and worth that he snapped, "there is a strained situation, after all, and yet the President has chosen to go off to his golf course."

However, General Eisenhower's love of the game was noted before his presidency, even outside of the United States. In one January 14, 1946 article in the *Toronto Globe and Mail* discussed his game in an article headlined *Eisenhower Modest About Golf Count*:

> Gen. Dwight D. Eisenhower has revealed himself a very modest golfer in accepting the invitation of the Royal and Ancient Golf Club of St. Andrews, Scotland to become an honorary life member.

> "I trust," he wrote, "that my performance as a golfer will not be publicized by my Scottish friends, as they would disown me at once."

That article hardly reflected the reality of how deeply ingrained the Sport of Presidents would become with Eisenhower. Most presidents have a signature *use*

for the game: some use it to broker deals on neutral territory, while others to connect with the people; however, Eisenhower's contribution is that he turned the
very game itself into his own *trademark*. He reset the notion of what the presidential sport would be, and it is fitting that a general would do so after the world
emerged from a tumultuous war.

When Eisenhower was elected to the highest office, one of the biggest stories
swirling around him was *golf:* the people and the press alike were *happy* that a
golfing president was in the White House again, and stories explored that very
angle. As the November 24, 1952 edition of the *Madera Tribune* noted:

> One of Eisenhower's Washington problems is going to be a golf course.
> He can't play on an ordinary course—too many sightseers, autograph
> hunters, job hunters. There's a beautiful public course just below the
> While House run by the national parks, but it's too public. And exclu-
> sive Burning Tree is far away. Perhaps the solution is for ex-ambassador
> Joe Davies to lend Ike his private golf course only ten minutes from the
> White House...Joe and Ike used to be bosom friends—at Potsdam—
> though they've differed vigorously of late...There hasn't been a golf-
> ing president in the White House since Harding...

With Eisenhower, golf became his newspeg: journalists felt obligated to angle
him that way. One UPI wire story on June 17, 1953, ran an article with the headline *Beat Eisenhower At Golf? Enjoy Thinks He Could:*

> The new U.S. Ambassador to Canada thinks he could beat his boss at
> golf, but he has never tried it.
>
> Ambassador-designate R. Douglas Stewart told newsmen at his first
> press conference here that he plays "a lot of golf." He wouldn't tell them
> his average score.
>
> "Could you beat President Eisenhower?" a reporter asked.
>
> "I think I could," the 67-year-old Chicagoan said.

Golf was a safe buffer, and reporters were more than happy to use it. As Roosevelt's contributions made golf part of middle-class life, and Eisenhower's love of
the game translated in a vastly different way than Taft or Harding's image to the

public. People could feel closer to the Commander in Chief, and golf was the common interest.

And often, press reports framed Eisenhower's doings in such a way that was relatable to the public, as the April 22, 1953, *Globe and Mail* noted under the section *Back to Work*:

> President Eisenhower flew back to the capital late today after a nine-day Georgia vacation during which he regained for the United States the initiative in the world "peace offensive," won a brief bout with food poisoning, and finally got his golf score under 90 for the first time since becoming president.

Other times, the stories also showed the difference between the perks of a golfing president to the rest of the public as the *Globe and Mail* noted in an April 4, 1953 article:

> Five Augusta firms have been asked to bid not later than Monday on the construction of a two-storey cabin at the Augusta National Golf Club. The building is to be used as a home by President Eisenhower when he visits Augusta.

Even after Eisenhower left office, press reports continued to report on his golfing. The *New York Times* had a headline in their November 20, 1966 piece *Eisenhower Golfs in Georgia*:

> Former President Dwight D. Eisenhower rested with friends today before putting in a round of golf under a bright sun at the golf course here.

It was an echo of a February 18, 1956 article headlined *Eisenhower Golfs In Georgia Drizzle; Does 9 Holes in 47; President Displays Good Form in His First Golf Since Heart Attack*:

> President Eisenhower confessed today to being "a little frightened of myself" as he played nine holes of golf for the first time since his heart attack Sept. 24.

In fact, the *Times* had no shortage of such headlines:

•Eisenhower, Out on Porch, Talks About Playing Golf; EISENHOWER SAYS HE IS 'JUST FINE' (November 21, 1965)

•Eisenhower in South For a Rest and Golf; Eisenhower Flies to Golf Course In Georgia, Seeking to Break 90 (February 27, 1953)

•Eisenhower Recalled as Anxious Golfer (April 10, 1969)

•Eisenhower Golfs on British Links (August 14, 1962)

•Eisenhower Shuns Golf (February 26, 1961)

•Eisenhower in Augusta for 'Sunshine and Golf (October 28, 1965)

•Eisenhower Plays Golf (July 26, 1959)

•Eisenhower in Coast Resort for Golf and Recuperation (January 8, 1967)

•Eisenhower Starts Golf Holiday (November 25, 1962)

•Eisenhower Golfs (October 26, 1958)

•Eisenhower Plays Golf (November 5, 1959)

•Eisenhower Plays Golf (April 3, 1960)

•Eisenhower Plays Golf (August 4, 1959)

•Eisenhower Plays Golf (July 12, 1959)

•Eisenhower Plays Golf (June 11, 1959)

•Eisenhower Plays Golf (February 12, 1961)

•Eisenhower Plays Golf (May 31, 1959)

•Eisenhower Plays Golf (August 19, 1960)

•Eisenhower Golfs (October 30, 1960)

•Eisenhower 'Mulligan Dedicates Golf Course (July 9, 1963)

•No Eisenhower Golf D-Day to V-E Day; White House Says Eisenhower Did Not Golf D-Day to V-E Day (November 6, 1959)

• EISENHOWER HAS COLD; Unable to Resume Golf Game at California Resort

At Palm Springs; confined to cottage with cold (February 17, 1961)

• EISENHOWER GOLFS, SIGNS PRIVATE BILLS (April 11, 1956)

And that is a small sampling of Eisenhower golf stories from the Times during his presidency (and this is not even an exhaustive list of the *Eisenhower Plays Golf* headline), and well after it. It was a consistent routine, and nothing stopped Eisenhower, not even food poisoning or a more serious affliction such as a heart attack.

Yet in all the articles about his golfing, few mentioned how golf helped Eisenhower move up social circles. As author Jeffrey Frank noted in 2013, Eisenhower parlayed the game to create a very elite inner circle:

> Eisenhower maintained a few old friendships from his army days, but he was more drawn to his new ones from America's business elite, with whom he spent hours playing golf and bridge, competing furiously at clubs like Augusta National...

If Taft and Harding made golf a craze, Eisenhower upped the ante to mania. His love for the game felt as if it were something out of a situation comedy's "bible", where every episode would revolve around his golf game, and there were no shortage of angles and antics: he had even thrown his club at his personal physician when one game was not going well and frustrated him. But the press was a constant presence and were the president's personal social media feed. For example, the October 23, 1960 edition of the *Evening Star* discussed the accolades for the Golfer in Chief:

> President Eisenhower was given a birthday and farewell party at Burning Tree Club last Saturday night and presented with two-lifetime gifts: (1) Continued membership in the club and (2) The Eisenhower Golf Fellowship.

> The latter, which was handsomely inscrolled in leather binding, gives him the lifetime privilege of selecting every one to three years a young officer in the armed services to become an honorary member of the club for that period. The recipient of the plush privilege must be below the rank of general officer and must, of course, be something of a golfer.

His devotion was contagious outside the U.S. with the *Arizona Post* relaying such details in an April 15, 1960 article:

> Last year there was a long essay in Sports Illustrated on sports in Israel, with the interesting observation that golf was coming to the land of working and pioneering people. As a matter of fact, it was clearly stated that golf had a better chance for popularity than baseball. Americans, by and large, couldn't understand that, but in the age of Eisenhower, golf has become a major sport and so it isn't too shocking that golf is moving into Israel, for it is.

However, not everyone was enthralled with the weekly routine of the Golf President. In one *This Week* article from the *Evening Star* on May 30, 1954, writer Merriman Smith dared asked the question *Does Eisenhower play too much Golf?* The article was an interesting take on the question:

> He plays about once a week, plus three golfing vacations a year. No GOLFER, with the possible exception of Ben Hogan, has as many volunteer score-keepers as President Eisenhower. Most of the people who keep track of Hogan, stroke by stroke, do so out of love of the game well played or their admiration for a champion. This, however, is not always the case with Mr. Eisenhower's coast-to-coast gallery.

The article seemed to be damning of the president:

> His political opponents, professional and amateur, keep books on the Chief Executive's game wherever he goes. They're not interested in what he shoots, but how many times he plays.

> A statement by Senator Wayne Morse of Oregon is a recent example. Senator Morse told the Senate that it was time the President "showed more interest in increasing employment and less interest in lowering his golf score."

> Some Eisenhower critics believe they can reap political hay by storing up statistics to support their claim that he spends too much time away from his job. There also are quite a number of private citizens who agree.

However, a twist would explain that the golf was part of a wellness strategy:

These people may not know that the President's doctor is after him constantly to play more golf, spend more time away from the hottest seat in America the high-backed chair behind T.R.'s old desk at 1600 Pennsylvania Avenue.

It was not the only article on the subject of *too much golf.* The *Evening Star* had such a piece on October 18, 1959, with the snarky headline *Has Ike Turned Pro?*:

Everybody knows that golf is President Eisenhower's favorite pastime. But some folks down in Washington think the President may have gone overboard or at least out-of-bounds in his devotion to the divots. Visitors at the Congressional Country Club, only 12 miles from the White House, claim they have seen the Chief Executive playing sneak rounds without his usual posse of Secret Service men. To thicken the mystery, these eyewitnesses allege the phantom Eisenhower swings like a Byron Nelson, smashes balls 265 yards off the tee, and jauntily tours the links in par.

Even more astonishing is the report that the President of the United States spends his morning standing around under a tree giving of lessons collecting the regular fee for a chore which, by no stretch of the Constitution, is a Presidential function. Why the rumors? It seems that the club pro, 61-year-old Willy Cox, is a ringer for the President of the United States. Wherever he goes, people, even admirals and Congressmen, mistake him for their leader.

But very few presidents who golf would escape the criticism of "golfing too much." It is an easy pot shot, but it is interesting that Eisenhower received his fair share from everyone from world leaders to regular citizens who weren't fans. Nevertheless, Eisenhower was a relatable president. He served in the army as did many others in that era, but it was his love of golf that connected to people. It made an extraordinary and rare elite — a president who was an army general — seem more average. It was a delicate balancing act and golf was an effective conduit for him.

Golf would follow Eisenhower to the end of his life and become entrenched in his legacy; however, the legacy of presidential golf would continue during the next and different kind of tumultuous decade from two presidents of a different political stripe.

Chapter Nine
On and Off Course

By the time the 1960s arrived, the zeitgeist and ortgeist were rapidly changing. The staidness of the Eisenhower years would eventfully give way to a more radical bend in the world with Baby Boomers providing a hardened youthful shift in the popular culture. This would be reflected in the Sport of Presidents: while the next two presidents would be golfers, how they used both the sport and its image would take a different direction.

It would seem intuitive that golf would fall out of favor to curry with the times; however, this was not the case. Golf was still a valuable asset that was emerging into an American force of its own and was a diverse and flexible game for a president to use. Taft, for instance, used golf to cultivate relationships with powerful industrialists, but the press would name drop those elites to the public. It created an image, yet the game served another purpose of hammering out the finer details on neutral ground. A very high-level meeting could be hidden right out in the open.

The scaffolding of the game was still sturdy with its own narrative: an affable president enthusiastically played with elites; another who could no longer play brought it to the common folk as they could aspire, and a third played it everywhere as his fellow Americans did the same. Above and below merged together, and of course, the story could not end there.

Because the times would still require a series of pivots to keep The Sport of Presidents relevant for the era.

John F. Kennedy campaigned by deriding his opponent Eisenhower for golfing, yet JFK himself was more than an able golfer; Lyndon Johnson, on the other hand, wasn't as deft of a golfer, but his use of the game to broker deals served its purpose well. Hence, golf became a vital venue to resolve political impasses: Kennedy smoothened, while Johnson cajoled and finessed.

President Kennedy's victory over Eisenhower was supposed to be a signal that perhaps golf was on its way out of the White House. To this day, many public perceptions align with that narrative. Author Robert Greene used this generation perception in his book *The 48 Laws of Power*:

> John F. Kennedy knew the dangers of getting lost in the past; he radically distinguished his presidency from that of his predecessor, Dwight D. Eisenhower, and also from the preceding decade, the 1950s, which Eisenhower personified. Kennedy, for instance, would not play the dull and fatherly game of golf— a symbol of retirement and privilege, and Eisenhower's passion. Instead, he played football on the White House lawn. In every aspect his administration represented vigor and youth, as opposed to the stodgy Eisenhower.

However, the truth is more complex than that, but let's take a look at why that perception took hold in the public first.

The origin of the divide was a case of optics: the victor wished to parlay Lajeunesse and a modern touch and golf seemed expendable. The *Toronto Globe and Mail* didn't question this narrative as they discussed Kennedy's victory on November 10, 1960:

> "But that doll Mrs. Kennedy should be a knockout as a First Lady. And I guess there'll be a bunch of kids around the White House. That should be popular. It will be nice to have a president with another hobby besides golf."

And yet when President Kennedy met with Eisenhower, their meeting place hinted that Presidential meetings are held out on the green. As the *Globe and Mail* noted on March 26, 1962:

> "It was a general discussion of the situation around the world," Pierre Slinger, the White House press secretary said later.

> "The President brought him up to date on a number of subjects, basically international."

The two men talked at former president Eisenhower's cottage on the 11th fairway of the El Dorado Country Club's golf course.

But while Kennedy promised no golfing in the White House, many in the press knew better and stated as much. The *Washington Evening Star* showed skepticism on January 4, 1961:

> The most dubious story of the year, we think, is the one that says John F. Kennedy will stop playing golf just as soon as he enters the White House on January 20. After all, although he has displayed a kind of allergy to being photographed on the links (a curious sensitivity that leaves us baffled), rumor hath it that he shoots a fine game that is said to be a shade or two better—in fact, several strokes better—than that of President Eisenhower and countless other Americans, including numerous friends of ours, who feel quite proud (even if not understandably so) of their respectably mediocre driving and putting.

There was no doubt that the press knew the score when it came to the Sport of Presidents:

> Mr. J. F. K., we are told, is exceptionally expert at this sort of thing when he switches to it from such altogether wholesome pursuits as swimming and touch football. Surely, when a man is good at anything—particularly golf—he ought to keep at it, and we doubt that he can tire of it, or brush it aside, just because he suddenly happens to become President of the United States. We are willing to bet that Mr. Kennedy, despite the news report, will take to the links after January 20. Anyhow, we hope so, because some of our friends tell us that nothing could be more relaxing even in those moments when it infuriates.

It is an interesting article that served an intriguing purpose: Kennedy was younger than Eisenhower and athletic: it would be difficult to believe that he wouldn't play and play better than Eisenhower. Kennedy did was not showy, however, and played with his own circle of partners: the press, however, were not invited or given hints of these outings, giving a very different impression than during the days of Eisenhower when the press would come along for the ride.

There were reasons for downplaying: with Eisenhower, golf had become on the border of farce: Kennedy quietly pulled it back from the brink. Kennedy played throughout his presidential campaign and after and could offer his biting humor while on the green, according to author Bill Adler:

During the heat of the 1960 Presidential campaign, Senator John Kennedy and a friend sought a few hours' respite on the golf course. On one short hole, Kennedy hit such a beautiful shot that it landed on the green and then began rolling straight toward the flag. His face registered pure terror until the ball barely missed the cup, roiling right by it. He turned to his partner in mock anger, "You're yelling for that damn ball to go in the hole and I am watching a promising political career coming to an end. If that ball had gone into that hole, in less than an hour the word would be out to the nation that another golfer was trying to get in the White House."

And Kennedy would play golf almost daily on the eve of his inauguration, according to author Thurston Clarke:

Kennedy filled the morning of January 12 with meetings, the afternoon with fishing and golf. On January 13, he met with Dean Rusk, played more golf, and fielded questions from reporters about his ambassadorial appointments.

And some of his golfing partners were well-known elites:

Billy Graham and Senator George Smathers of Florida arrived at noon to join Kennedy for lunch followed by a round of golf. Salinger had told the press this encounter between the nation's first Catholic president and its second most prominent Protestant clergyman (Norman Vincent Peale came first) would give Graham an opportunity to suggest some biblical verses for the inaugural address.

The shift would take the presidential sport to another level: there would be less public access, but the use of golf to conduct political, social, academic, and corporate meetings would still be in play. There would be strict limits to what the press could show the public. The *Washington Evening Star* let readers know about those limits in an April 4, 1961 article headlined *Kennedy Lefts Golf Curtain*:

President Kennedy permitted pictures to be taken of him on the golf course today—but not with a club in his hand. It was the first time since Mr. Kennedy's election as President that he has allowed any news pictures to be made of him on a golf course. Apparently, he doesn't want a picture of him swinging a golf club to get fixed in the public mind for

fear it will subject him to the kind of criticism that President Eisenhower's golfing brought from Democrats—including himself. Even
having the news photographers and some reporters standing around
watching him seemed to make Mr. Kennedy nervous.

The golfing ban soon became something of a punchline and fair-game fodder
for the press. Columnist Fletcher Knebel took a swing in the *Washington Evening
Star* on February 23, 1961:

> President Kennedy plays mid-week golf with Senator Smathers. That's
> the New Frontier spirit for you—hacking a trail through the wilderness
> to stake a claim on the country club vote.

The *San Bernardino Sun* also made an interesting observation on July 24, 1963:

> President Kennedy's refusal to permit photographers to snap an occa-
> sional photograph of him playing golf is somewhat amusing. This self-
> conscious penchant is an admission that he does play golf.

The people wanted a president open about golfing — it had become a way to
feel a kinship with the Commander in Chief. In a May 13, 1961, *Washington
Evening Star* article headlined *Kennedy Relaxes, Swims, Plays Golf In Palm Beach*,
the golf made its way to the presidential narrative once again — but this time
mixed in with other sports:

> President Kennedy kept the golf clubs and swim trunks handy today for
> another day of relaxation at links and pool.

> Swimming and golf, plus reports from Washington that always demand
> presidential time, once again were the main objective of the Kennedy
> day. The Chief Executive's four-day week end here beside the Atlantic
> is the closest thing to a vacation he has had since his inauguration.

> Christopher Dunphy, Palm Beach amateur, and Charles Spalding, New
> York banker, are the President's regular golfing partners. Various per-
> sons get the extra spot for a foursome. Mr. Kennedy decided to switch
> courses today, from the Palm Beach Country Club to the Breakers Club.

The article provided insight into who was the common inner golfing circle for
the president — and that there was a wild card placement. Unlike coverage about
Eisenhower which strictly focused on golf, after a shaky start, Kennedy realized

that golf was too important a symbol to squander, but *layering* the coverage to make more textured narrative could bring golf back into the picture, especially as Kennedy took advantage of the space to practice his game, according to author George Sullivan:

> Kennedy took advantage of the spacious White House South Lawn to practice his golf shots. He would place a doormat on the grass. Then, using a seven-, eight-, or nine-iron, he would hit one high-arching pitch shot after another.

As it became common knowledge that Kennedy played his fair share of the game, there were advantages to bringing it back into the picture. Golfing instructor Max Elbin saw Kennedy up close and described Kennedy's abilities the best in the 24 February 24, 1966 edition of the *Desert Sun:*

> "President Kennedy impressed me the most," said the youthful-looking, 45-year-old Maryland native over a cup of coffee at a midtown hotel. "He had a natural golf swing and, although he never had time to play more than nine holes at Burning Tree, he always kept the ball on the fairway." Elbin revealed that President Eisenhower shot mostly "in the mid 80's" when he used to play Burning Tree, "although one day he turned in a 79."

While Eisenhower loved the game, his manner was not quite like Kennedy's low-key approach:

> "Some of President Eisenhower's golfing partners used to give him the short putts, but he didn't like that at all," said Elbin. "He also used to hate to play through slower groups. He'd say, 'let the other people play first.' And, you know, every time he played through it affected his game."

Kennedy brought the element of *elegance,* and often humor into the equation. Author Bill Adler wrote about one of his golfing forays with Jackie:

> Once John Kennedy was playing the Hyannis Port golf course with his wife, Jackie. On the seventeenth hole, he watched her vainly try to blast her ball out of a sand trap, on each try the exasperating ball trickling back to her feet. "Open the face of the club," he called from his golf cart. "Follow through." But it was of no avail. Finally, he lost patience and,

taking the club from Jackie announced, "Let me show you." After a couple of fluid practice swings, he brought the club back gracefully, then swung it down powerfully into and through the sand. The ball rose a good two feet and dribbled mockingly back into the sand. Without losing his poise for a moment, Kennedy handed the club back to Jackie and said, "See, that's how you do it."

Kennedy provided polish to the image of the game, elevating it without the classism or snobbery. President Johnson, on the other hand, was less concerned with optics than with the efficiency of getting things done out on the green.

Lyndon Johnson, on the other hand, had no grace as a golfer, but he had the savvy to know he could negotiate deals and work away impasses on the golf course. His ground-breaking 1964 Civil Rights Act was negotiated on the golf course, and this was a breakthrough for the game: breakthrough policies could be hammered out on the green.

Johnson also golfed with former president Eisenhower in 1968: he toured military installations near Palm Springs, California, and decided to cap off the trip with a game. The image became instantly iconic. Another image of him playing at Ramsay Air Force Base is another highly recognizable one, though his swing looked more as if he wished to bludgeon the ball rather than merely hit it.

Johnson didn't shy away from the game, though he took full advantage of it. It was an extension of the Oval Office, and knowing the finer points of the actual game was secondary as the *Atlantic* noted in July 1973:

> He took up golf, puttering around courses in Fredericksburg, and on trips to Mexico. One day, playing with a few aides and friends, Johnson hit a drive into the rough, retrieved it, and threw the ball back on the fairway. "Are you allowed to do that?" one of the wives whispered to a Secret Service agent. "You are," he replied, "if you play by LBJ rules."

The game was secondary to the goal: powerful people want to be seen with the most powerful one. To Johnson, golf was a pretense, yet by passing the Civil Rights Act on a golf course was a powerful message: the act itself banned segregation based on race, including golf courses.

Yet not everyone was enthralled with the president's methods, such as an article in the *New York Times* on April 26, 1964:

Stan Musial, the resident physical-fitness Chief of the Government, might also help. Lately the President has shown a vague interest in golf, but this makes things even worse. Golf is a plague, invented by the Calvinistic Scots as a punishment for man's sins, and nobody has yet found anybody in Washington the President can beat.

While it almost seemed as if *The Sport of Presidents* took a break in the 60s, nothing could have been further than the truth: Johnson used the golf course to bring in the Civil Rights Act, and the method became the stuff of legends. That golf was instrumental in bringing about progressive change seemed like a crowning glory, but presidential golf's story hardly ends there. Each president had brought something new to the game's mystique, but most presidents did not have an established family legacy of the game — save for two: George H.W. Bush and his son George W. Bush.

Chapter Ten
The Dynasty, Part One

The Bush family's legacy in golf is an interesting and storied affair, and it is fascinating that of all the presidents who golfed, the Bushes were the only ones whose family was firmly entrenched in the game. Because of this added layer, it is helpful to discuss the Bush Family's roots in the game before discussing the two presidents who were proud and able golfers.

It is no surprise that golf is so ingrained in the family. As the *Houston Chronicle* noted in a December 7, 2018 tribute to George H.W. Bush:

> He loved the game and the values it stood for — patience, perseverance, accountability, and respect. He loved to be around it. He loved to play it. He loved the people who played it.

The grandson of former USGA president George Herbert Walker, who created the Walker Cup, and son of past USGA president Prescott Bush, Bush played baseball at Yale, but honed his golf game and won the Cape Arundel Club Championship in 1947.

The roots of the dynasty began with the well-to-do George Herbert Walker, a prominent banker, and businessman, who interestingly enough, was an amateur heavyweight boxer, winning the Missouri title while he was studying law at Washington University. He, like future generations, would be highly athletic and excel at numerous sports; however, each would make the greatest contribution to golf.

His dedication to the game helped propel him to USGA president in 1920 and had an impressive 5 handicap. Of all the line of this powerful family, he remains the best golfer, but his best-known contribution is the prestigious Walker Cup.

The Walker Cup was founded in 1922 when Walker created the idea to create an international amateur competition and offered to donate the trophy. The first game was played at the National Golf Links, which had another connection to the family as discussed below. As the USAG noted on September 5, 2013:

The idea for the Match occurred to Walker after he and a contingent from the USGA traveled to St. Andrews, Scotland, for meetings with the Royal & Ancient Golf Club, the governing body of golf for the world outside of the U.S. and Mexico. Walker and other Americans took the opportunity to also compete in the British Amateur at Muirfield. After returning to the States, Walker thought the meetings with the R&A were fruitful and wanted to see them renewed. Later that year he proposed a plan during a USGA Executive Committee meeting for golfing countries to compete in a team championship in conjunction with the meetings. He even offered to donate the trophy, which was dubbed the United States Golf Association International Challenge Trophy.

The golfing tradition continued in the family with Connecticut senator Prescott S. Bush who also was a devoted golfer along with his wife Dorothy Walker Bush. It should be no surprise that Prescott Bush frequently golfed with President Eisenhower: a foreshadowing of things to come for the Bush family. As George H.W. Bush recounted later to the Golf Channel:

"My dad was a very low-handicap player, and he was in the Senate when Ike [Dwight Eisenhower] was president...And he played with Eisenhower quite a bit. Through the eyes of my dad, I got the insight into being a president. Not on issues, but on what made him relax and what kind of a good sport he was. I vicariously learned about golf because my dad used to play with Ike."

And it would be Eisenhower who extended the invitation as author Mickey Herskowitz explained:

That winter and spring Eisenhower began inviting Prescott to play golf with him. The president was a devout golfer. One of his early actions as president had been to have a putting green installed on the White House lawn. Heading for the links was a valued escape for him, but it also could be a valuable opportunity for anyone, legislator or businessman, who qualified to be invited to play along.

Prescott Bush's game was the stuff of legends: and to have the Golf President as one of your golfing companions merely added to the mythos, and it would be a hard act to top, as his grandson and former President George W. Bush recounted in his book *41* in 2014:

> My grandfather's most influential friend in the capital was President Dwight Eisenhower. One key to developing the friendship was my grandfather's golf game. Ike loved to play golf, and there was no better golfer in the Senate than Prescott Bush. Ike especially liked that the Senator, unlike most politicians, refused to let the President win. Years later, my brother Marvin invited me to play a round at the Burning Tree Club in Maryland, one of the places where my grandfather and President Eisenhower used to play. Marv introduced me to our caddie, who told me he had carried the bag for my grandfather decades earlier. After watching me play about five holes, he delivered his assessment. "Your grandfather was a hell of a lot better than you are," he said. "He could shape it left, shape it right, make it move. When you hit it good, you're just lucky." The fellow wasn't afraid to speak the truth.

The senator, like Walker, was a member of Cape Arundel (in Kennebunkport, Maine), winning the club championship eight times. It is an impressive achievement, and the Bush family is as close to golfing royalty as one can get, but it is not the only familial connection: steal and railroad industrialist Samuel P. Bush was Prescott's father who was also a supporter of the game. He was one of four co-founders of the fabled Scioto Country Club in Columbus, Ohio, a private club that opened in 1916 and designed by famed golf course designer Donald Ross who was a golfer himself. It was the first place where legend Jack Nicklaus honed his skills, and Bobby Jones won the U.S. Open in 1926.

The idea for Scioto came to Bush and his companions after visiting the National Golf Links of America in 1913. Inspired, they built the course on leased farmland while Prescott was attending Yale. As the USGA noted in 2018:

> Prescott, home for the summer from Yale, where he was a member of the golf team, worked on the construction crew, earning $1 per day. He was known to play Scioto often in a year or two after it opened in 1916. Following World War I, golf was an asset in his business and political careers.

Bush was a strong advocate and as PGA President, wrote an article entitled *1936 Seen as Big Golf Year in U. S./Business Improvement Fills Out Membership of Clubs Through Nation* that appeared in the *Bismarck Tribune* on February 3, 1936:

> Golfers may well look forward to the advent of 1936 with the expectation that it will be indeed a happy new year. The improvement in business and the better feeling that has accompanied it already are making a difference in the attitude of members toward their clubs and their golf games. Repeal of prohibition has likewise contributed to the greater enjoyment of clubs and to the revenue of the clubs from the sale of beverages. Club finances are in better shape, and getting better. Memberships are filling up, and the whole situation is becoming more normal and more pleasurable.

A month earlier, a longer version of the optimistic piece in the *Washington Evening Star* on January 3, 1936, with this passage:

> The game of golf is relatively free from controversy. There are no unhappy disputes raging and none appears on the horizon…

Golf officials note with satisfaction the continued growth of municipal golf. The public links championship, sponsored by the USGA [United States Golf Association], is the high spot in municipal golf links competition and serves to bring home to the growing army of public links players the importance of observing the rules of golf and the true spirit and line traditions of the game. Perhaps no game that is played by millions of our people is so capable as golf of developing the sense of sportsmanship, courtesy and consideration of the opponent.

When he made PGA President in 1934, it made national news, complete with a closeup of him looking stoic and swinging a club in a crisp white shirt. When he became a senator, his golfing made got the press talking as the *Santa Cruz Sentinel* did on November 18, 1952:

> If President-elect Eisenhower wants a good golfing companion in Washington, he will find him in Connecticut's new Republican Senator Prescott Bush. At 57, Bush still looks and is the 6-foot-4 athlete who played first base for Yale. He once shot a record-breaking 18-hole 66 in the U. S. Seniors golf tournament He is a good tennis player and swimmer; his

bass voice is better than most you hear in any 19th hole quartet and as a World War artillery captain he can swap tales with any soldier.

When the inevitable golf pairing of Bush and Eisenhower came to be, it made the news as well, including in the *San Bernardino Sun* on August 23, 1956:

President Eisenhower and Sen. Prescott Bush, a couple of pretty important Republicans, got together on this highlight day of the GOP national convention. But their minds strayed from politics a bit to golf. Bush called on the President to report officially that the convention unanimously had approved the party platform Tuesday night. The Connecticut senator was chairman of the committee which drafted the document. He spent about 10 or 15 minutes with the President, and told newsmen later the chief executive was "very well satisfied with the platform." NOW AS TO GOLF Then about golf Bush reported he had expressed regret that he couldn't stay a bit longer on the coast to play a round with Eisenhower after the convention at Cypress Point. The President plans to vacation there

With that illustrious scaffolding in place, it should be no surprise that not one, but two members of the Bush family reached the White House.

Chapter Eleven

The Dynasty, Part Two

It is interesting that both George H.W. Bush and his son George W. Bush share a presidency and a devotion to golf in common, but how each man used the sport while in office is a study of contrasts. George Bush Senior seemed destined to the White House given his father's friendship with the Golf President, while his namesake son made symbolic use of the sport itself.

Both presidents were cultivated for the office, and it is the game itself that gave the air to the narrative. While JFK tried to create the air by downplaying his golfing prowess, the Bush family made no secret of it. The family contribution to the sport is profound. Bush 41 had a reverence to the game as it was entrenched in his illustrious family's lore, and he overtly linked the game's lessons with his family and the positive traits it instilled in him. He could weave an intricate web with the game as he painted a picture of an upper-crust American family. It was a precious element to be kept at all costs.

However, while Bush 43 was passed the torch, yet he did something utterly unique: he turned the game into an element that could be sacrificed, albeit temporarily for the greater good. Because of these divergent views of the sport, it is important to look at the contexts of each narrative in a different manner entirely.

At the core of Bush 41's narrative of golf, is its ability to create a better person. Learning golf imparted more than just skill or strategy: it brought in emotional literacy. This shift in focus is an interesting one that aligned with his kinder, gentler nation sentiments. Bush explained how golf built character in several media interviews. As the USGA website on December 1, 2018, noted:

> "Golf has meant a lot to me. It means friendship, integrity and character," Bush said upon receiving the Bob Jones Award. "I grew up in a family that was lucky enough to have golf at the heart of it for a while.

My father was a scratch player and my mother also was a good golfer.
It's a very special game."

However, this was no attempt at adding a folksy touch, particularly given his
background and position as Congressman, U.S. Ambassador to the United Nations, CIA Director, Vice President, and then President. Bush's golfing partners
seemed very similar to President Taft's. It was a way to mingle and network with
the global elite. As the *Houston Chronicle* mentioned in a December 7, 2018 article:

> Back in the 1960s — even before he was elected Congressman for Dis-
> trict 7 in 1967 — Bush was a member at Houston County Club. As his
> career moved him to Washington D.C., as CIA director, Ambassador to
> China and Vice President, he would still find time when he was in town
> to play a round with Nolan Ryan or former Astros manager Hal Lanier.

The article went on to discuss the President's contributions to the game:

> But Bush's influence in the game was much wider than just personal
> moments.

> Not long after he left office, he threw his support behind the President's
> Cup, which debuted in 1994, as the honorary chairman, then pulled
> President Bill Clinton on board as well. He was a staple at both of those
> team events, driving around with the teams.

> He also jumped on board with the First Tee in 1997 as honorary chair-
> man and Houston was one of the cities that helped jump-start the pro-
> gram.

Even Bush's Vice President Dan Quayle was tutored in the sport while in office, according to a December 7, 1991 article in the *Globe and Mail:*

> David Leadbetter transformed Nick Faldo into a golfer who has won
> four major championships since 1987. He helped Seve Ballesteros to a
> magnificent season this year. And now Leadbetter faces another chal-
> lenge: Today he's giving his first lesson to U.S. Vice President Dan
> Quayle.

"Quayle's people called my office and told me he'd like to come down [today]," Leadbetter said…"I told them I could fit him in with two others. They said that wouldn't do for security reasons."

It took some presidential cajoling to get things in motion, however:

Leadbetter changed his plans, as instructors are wont to do when the White House calls. The schedule now calls for Leadbetter to work with Quayle this morning, then play 18 holes with him and a friend this afternoon.

But Bush made serious decisions on the links, and often, to know where he would take his policies could be gleaned there. The *Toronto Star* had made note of it in a January 1, 1991 article:

Bush has moved about 20 per cent of the U.S. armed forces to the bleak deserts of northeastern Saudi Arabia. He has filled the Saudi airstrips with fighters and bombers. He has persuaded Canada, Britain and France, as well as Egypt and Syria to send troops to the gulf. He has persuaded the Soviets to condemn their long time Iraqi clients.

His detestation of Saddam, frequently vented over golf carts and at military bases, seems total.

Getting out of Kuwait is not enough, he has said.

Bush was not jovial on the course when it came to serious global issues. The *Santa Cruz Sentinel* also revealed how golf was a presidential omen on August 20, 1990:

The president's vacation has stopped being fun. George Bush is going through the motions of recreation, grimly determined not to be held captive in the White House. His aides, knowing his stubborn side, do not press him to cut short his 25-day holiday, even though some believe that it would be more appropriate if Bush returned to Washington, for more than brief visits, as he did Sunday. And they would prefer it if he stopped speaking to reporters about the chilling Persian Gulf crisis while sitting in his golf cart.

And the mood was a serious one even on the links:

"It looks horrible," one Bush adviser said of the scenes of the president fishing and golfing and running, juxtaposed with others of frightened families of the Americans detained in Iraq and Kuwait and the frightened families of troops leaving for the Middle East. "The president doesn't even seem to be having fun racing around the golf course," the official added. "It's almost as though he's on some driven mission." Bush has been so determined to keep playing that he went golfing one day when it was raining so hard that the Cape Arundel golf course was closed to less important and less determined golfers. The course was so soaked that when his ball landed in a flooded sand trap, the president had to ask Ken Raynor, the club's golf pro and his regular partner, if he should play it or count it as a water hazard and take a penalty stroke.

While Eisenhower's golfing was itself the subject of news articles, with Bush, there was always some global crisis mixed in. It was a singular and distinctive image. The *Boston Globe* had such a scene in an August 13, 1991 story:

Publicly, at least, Bush is maintaining a hands-off policy in dealing with the hostage-takers. But he is also promoting a scenario under which the hostages in Lebanon would be released at the same time as all other hostages held by other countries are freed.

Coincidence or not, Bush's idea is similar to that demanded by the hostage-takers in a letter made public yesterday.

The Islamic Jihad said in its letter that it wanted "the release of all detainees throughout the world."

Bush, teeing off for a 6:20 a.m. golf game near his vacation home, sounded a strikingly similar theme, saying that "there's been a framework for a deal for a long time in terms of people releasing all hostages."

It should be no surprise then that for Bush, golf was a way to work through serious problems, and needed to be solved expediently. No wonder he had his own version of the game, dubbed "Speed golf." His golf was not unlike a Ramones concert in that regard. What it meant for other players was explained in a December 2, 2018 piece from *Golf Pro Now*:

"You put your track shoes on when you played with him," Tour player Hale Irwin remarked. Bush from time to time declared that anybody who wanted to play golf with him better be prepared to finish an 18-hole round in no more than three hours.

His version of the game reflected his own temperament according to an article in *Golfweek* on Feb. 15, 1995:

"I'm always in a hurry…The faster, the better. It's my personality. I like to get a lot of things done during the day, so standing around on a golf course doesn't suit me."

Golf accentuated his active mindset. It displayed his temperament and his drive as it was meant to prove his age was not a factor in his essence. The *Austin American Statesman* replayed his methods in an August 27, 1989 story:

President Bush's record time for playing 18 holes at Cape Arundel Golf Club used to be two hours 20 minutes. That was until a few days ago, when he pushed the throttle full tilt on his golf cart and, with a full contingent of Secret Service agents in tow, zoomed around the course.

Now the record is one hour and 51 minutes.

He wasn't shuffling on the green. His message was on point with his golf game:

Speed may not be the aim for most golfers, but it's important to Bush. There's no other way he could cram his other recreational interests into very little time.

During a three-week stay at his seaside summer home, Bush has set a new pace for presidential relaxation, supersonic style.

Other presidents have participated in sports — Jimmy Carter jogged, Gerald Ford golfed and played tennis and a youthful John Kennedy sparked a fitness craze in the 1960s — but the man who is the fourth oldest to be inaugurated president is evolving into the most relentless sports activist yet to occupy the White House.

He was at his best when he was active, and golf was his symbol of vitality:

Such a daily schedule might add up to total exhaustion for many Americans. Bush last week called it the "total vacation."

"He says it clears his mind," says Bush's press secretary, Marlin Fitzwater. "He's always been that way."

Despite his youthful energy, or because of it, he was often chided for spending too much time on the golf course — a common criticism that came from detractors of any president. As one December 7, 1991 article in the *Globe and Mail* sniffed that "political observers…criticized Bush for spending too much time on the golf course."

And yet he was accessible to journalists from the course and aware of global events. The golf course was always an extension of the Oval Office, and a far healthier venue than an enclosed room cut off from the rest of the world. Somehow, a president is expected to be locked down and not move in order to think. Golf liberates more than tethers and it explains why so many U.S. presidents take up the sport According to the *Montreal Gazette* on ay 29, 1990, Bush could hold a press conference, be monitoring a major world development, and take in a game:

Bush told the crowd that as he prepares to meet with Gorbachev, "things have changed dramatically; there's no question that we have a better chance now for a lasting world peace."

"But there are still some enormous problems out there," he said. "And this country must remain strong."

Bush has made an effort in the days before the summit to emphasize that Gorbachev — despite his problems — is a powerful world leader who has the authority to make deals with the United States.

"I think we spend too much time trying to figure out how long a leader in any country will be there (in power)," Bush said, answering reporter's questions at a country club before a final round of golf.

His post-presidency golf-playing also made the news. When he played, it was usually in A-list company as the February 4, 1994 edition of the *Hamilton Spectator* noted:

Former President George Bush and comedian Bill Murray both went into the gallery on the first hole they played yesterday in the AT&T Pebble Beach National Pro-Am golf tournament.

Bush did it by accident, hitting his second shot into the huge crowd lining the fairway. A spectator was clipped but unhurt by a glancing blow.

Whether Murray's journey outside the ropes was an accident remains to be determined. In any event, the comedian, completely unabashed by some criticism from golf's hierarchy, continued to take his act into the gallery and roll around on the ground.

Murray and Bush played at Spyglass Hill, by far the most difficult of the three Monterey Peninsula courses used for this unique event.

Bush had a deep reverence for the game: it was his constant companion. He understood the game and its strategic benefits and was an accomplished golfer with enviable accolades. Cape Arundel renamed their clubhouse 41 House in 2011 as an homage to George 41. Bush was also inducted into the World Golf Hall of Fame in 2011, but it was hardly his only lofty golfing honor:

- Club championship at Cape Arundel (1947).

- PGA of America's Distinguished Service Award (1997)

- USGA's Bob Jones Award (2008)

- PGA Tour's Lifetime Achievement Award (2009)

- Honorary chairman of the Presidents Cup (1996)

- Honorary Member of the PGA

- Honorary chairman of the USGA Museum and Archives President's council

- Honorary chairman of The First Tee (1997-2011)

But it was more than just honors. He had always maintained that golf helped in other ways as well. There was solace in golf after his defeat to fellow golfer Bill Clinton as the *Globe and Mail* recounted on December 3, 1992:

Since his electoral defeat, Mr. Bush has retreated from the usual White House schedule and taken two holidays, during which he has been seen trudging, grim-faces, over golf courses.

Yet golf built a bridge to the rival who defeated him as the *Atlantic* recounted on December 2, 2018:

> Clinton and the elder Bush soon began hanging out stateside as well. They played golf together in a charity tournament with the pro golfer Greg Norman, and Bush routinely checked in on Clinton during his health scare in early 2005.

By the time George 43 came to the Oval Office, he was already established as an able golfer and golfed with his then-president father. As the *New York Times* recounted in an August 18, 1989 article, even on the golf course, the future George 43 would see first-hand what would wait for him eleven years later:

> Mr. Bush, who is vacationing here for three weeks with his family, had a national security briefing this morning from Robert Gates, the deputy national security adviser. Later, after a boating and fishing expedition, he was briefed on the developments.
>
> The Administration is working on legislation to carry out the economic aid plan that the President took to Eastern Europe last month. It would give $100 million to Poland, and $25 million to Hungary to encourage free enterprise.
>
> The President was asked about Poland as he played golf with his son, George W. Bush, at the Cape Arundel Golf Club on a beautiful, breezy afternoon. "No comment," said the President, who is usually willing to chat to reporters about his game but not about foreign affairs. Asked how his vacation was going, he replied, "Now we're talking."

However, while there was a family tie progressing, the focus would soon be on Bush 43 himself. It was an interesting shift in the illustrious narrative, as was the case in a January 13, 1999 piece in the *Austin American Statesman:*

> Gov. George W. Bush planned to play golf today with two presidents — Argentina's Carlos Menem and former President George Bush. "His

father called and asked if he could make time to play golf with the president of Argentina, who is a close friend of President Bush's," said Karen Hughes, the governor's spokeswoman.

Once he was president, Bush 43 seemed to take a more light-hearted approach to the game as the *Los Angeles Times* noted on July 4, 2001:

George W. Bush went golfing for the first time as president, following his predecessor Bill Clinton's practice of taking a do- over mulligan shot and enjoying the perk of certain victory.

"It's called 'president wins,'" Bush said as he finished his round at Andrews Air Force Base by pocketing the ball after missing a putt for par 5.

With a weekend of golf coming up at the Bush family compound in Kennebunkport, Maine, the president sought to brush up on his game.

The Melbourne *Herald Sun* added more about that first post-presidential victory game on July 5, 2001:

He took a mulligan off the first tee, sending two shots in quick succession off to the left.

After that, he turned and joked to onlookers: "Exactly where you want to be".

"I haven't played since I've been President," Mr. Bush said. "I've been working too hard."

At the 18th hole, Mr. Bush, appearing in good spirits, summed up his game to reporters. He said he had seven pars, "no birdies, a fair amount of bogeys, a couple of double bogeys, but fun was had by all".

"Did you see my drive on this last hole?" he asked. "I crushed it, but unfortunately the game is more than driving."

This showed a vastly different approach to the game than of his father: to the father, golf was a serious business to be woven in with international business. To the son, this was fun, and something to be left until after-hours.

Yet that game made international news, with different outlets looking at different angles. The *Times of London* chimed in on the game on July 5, 2001:

His golfing partners say that his most effective weapon on the course is his constant stream of teasing remarks to other players. "I've never seen him when he wasn't needling somebody he's with," George Gist, director of golf operations at Barton Creek course in Austin, said.

A President may be able to play just how he wants in office, but once he leaves the White House his golfing habits may be subject to scrutiny. In a November interview with Golf Digest, Mr. Clinton insisted that he did not bend the rules as much as his critics claimed. "My mulligans are way overrated," he said.

But after September 11, the game of golf would take a different meaning.

It was then Bush who made a decision not to golf: for him, it was levity and escapism, and it clashed with world events. This sacrifice of the game gave the presidential version of the sport a new twist: it was a precious commodity to give it up was a sign of respect for those in the line of fire.

However, not everyone was impressed as the May 15, 2008 edition of the *Guardian* pointed out:

> George Bush has angered U.S. war veterans by declaring that out of solidarity with those who made the ultimate sacrifice in Iraq he decided to make his own sacrifice: giving up golf.
>
> ...[T]he president said he took the decision because of the war. "I don't want some mom whose son may have recently died to see the commander in chief playing golf. I feel I owe it to the families to be in solidarity. And I think playing golf during a war just sends the wrong signal."
>
> Brandon Friedman, a veteran U.S. infantry officer who served in both Iraq and Afghanistan, told the Press Association: "Thousands of Americans have given up a lot more than golf for this war. For President Bush to imply that he somehow stands in solidarity with families of American soldiers by giving up golf is disgraceful. It's an insult to all Americans and a slap in the face to our troops' families."

After he left office after his second term, Bush resumed the game and made news in the process for his own more modest achievements. In the March 20, 2019 edition of *Golf Digest* discussed one:

[T]he news shared on Wednesday by Dubya will not only bring a smile to many golf fans faces—but it'll also provide hope for anyone who has never made a hole in one. The former president made the first ace of his life, at age 72, and he posted the picture to his Instagram account. 2019 ... what a time to be alive!

According to his caption, the hole-in-one came at the par-3 12th hole at Trinity Forest Golf Club, which will host the AT&T Byron Nelson for the second time this May, a week before the PGA Championship.

Bush 43 had used the *absence* of golf to show solidarity and was one of the few golfing presidents not to be accused of golfing too much. Still, for the Bush Dynasty, his road to the White House was paved through a golf course: each generation made progress on the links, and the game opened a path to the highest office in a way no other family before had done.

Chapter Twelve
A Swing from the Right

The Bush presidents are hardly the only modern-day Republican presidents who golfed. Richard Nixon, Gerald Ford, Ronald Reagan, and Donald Trump all played the Sport of Presidents. In fact (as in the case of Democratic presidents), most of these presidents (save for one) had presidential rivals who did *not* golf. The golfer will beat the non-golfer: Ronald Regan defeated non-golfers Jimmy Carter and Walter Mondale, George Bush 41 defeated non-golfer Michael Dukakis. George Bush 43 defeated both Al Gore and John Kerry, the non-golfers. It is one of the most reliable barometers of campaign victory. When it comes to selecting a presidential candidate, golf skills are a definite asset.

Golf is part of the presidential package, and each Republican president brought something else to the game's mythos: Nixon darkly persevered, Ford championed, Trump taunted, and Reagan accentuated.

Very rarely does a golf-playing presidential candidate lose to one who does not, but Gerald Ford is a rare exception, and his love of the game became a sticking point during the 1976 presidential race against Democratic contender Jimmy Carter. While attacks on a candidate's golf game are usually fair game for a rival, this time, it was within his own party that Ford heard complaints as the August 23, 1976 edition of the *Desert Sun* revealed:

> The President spent the weekend playing golf and tennis and. according to Press Secretary Ron Nessen. plans to "take it easy for one more day." That decision drew criticism from his running mate, Sen Robert Dole, R-Kan. In a *Time* magazine interview, Dole said of the President, "with eight weeks to go, he has to be very aggressive. I don't know how you can do much else but go to Georgia the first day after the convention and work your way up. With him going to Vail for a week that's 15 per cent down the drain."

Gerald Ford was a devoted golfer and had been part of his legacy. His golfing made the news, even when he was Vice President, as it did in the *Santa Cruz Sentinel* on April 18, 1974:

Vice President Gerald Ford, disappointed with a Republican election setback in Michigan, hoped to boost the re-election prospects of a California GOP congressman today. Ford was scheduled to interrupt his Palm Springs golfing vacation to campaign for Rep. Burt L. Talcott, a five-term congressman from Salinas who faces a tough race in a reapportioned district that' is a Democratic target in 1974. Ford played golf on the private nine-hole course of the Walter Annenberg estate at Palm Springs Wednesday.

In fact, one of his first forays as president was to speak at the opening of the World Golf Hall of Fame on September 11, 1974:

I can only say, regardless of which sport, I think, whether it is golf, professional or college football, or any one of the other wonderful athletic areas of competition, so much is added to America's society by the things that you learn and the things that you do. So, I am always a willing participant in anything that involves athletics. I think it is great and wholesome, not only for the United States but the world. And, naturally, I wish to compliment and congratulate Don and Bill and those who had the vision and the foresight. I am sure you realize what a thrill it is for a weekend golfer like myself to walk the same fairways today with Byron Nelson, Gene Sarazen, Ben Hogan, Sam Snead, Arnold Palmer, Jack Nicklaus, Gary Player, Patty Berg. I always have idols in athletics, and I don't apologize for it now. These are the kind of idols that I think are good and wholesome for America.

During his tenure as president, there would be a textured and almost surreal essence to the stories. The pastiche of elements made for surprising reading, as it did in the August 11, 1975 edition of the *Desert Sun*:

Ford and his wife, Betty, watched Betty's interview on CBS TV's "60 Minutes," During the interview, she said that she "wouldn't be surprised" if her daughter Susan, 18, decided to have an affair. White House press secretary Ron Nessen told reporters Ford did not directly comment on his wife's views but said the President has "always taken the position that Mrs. Ford should speak her mind." Ford expected to begin a daily regimen of swimming, tennis, and golf starting today with

Alan Greenspan, chairman of the Council of Economic Advisers, as one of his golfing companions.

Ford seemed to channel Eisenhower in some ways for his love of the game, but it was his abilities that gave him the better press. Praise for his golf game came from the celebrity A-list, according to a December 21, 1975 article in the *Santa Cruz Sentinel:*

> Of all the golfing presidents, none could match Gerald Ford's distance off the tee but John F. Kennedy was the best striker of the ball and Dwight D. Eisenhower was the fiercest competitor, says Bob Hope. "Richard Nixon is like Ike "in his enthusiasm for the game," the comedian added. "He never had the natural athletic instincts of, say, Kennedy or Ford, but he got his game down to a 14 handicap through sheer work and determination. He is very keen. I played with Lyndon Johnson only once. That was in Acapulco. I remember Darrell Royal, the Texas football coach, also played with us. LBJ didn't have much of a love or feel for the game."

Ford could be seen with an interesting assortment of golfing companions, ensuring press coverage, often quite positive. For instance, under the headline *Enthusiastic Welcome Given to President Ford* in the *Santa Cruz Sentinel* on March 31, 1975, his visit to California, he had managed to parlay golf into a cocktail party out on the links:

> Ford spent much of Sunday afternoon golfing at La Quinta Country Club with Earl "Red" Blaik, former West Point football coach, movie director Frank Capra and La Jolla. Calif., business executive Leon Parma.

However, his golfing also got him into trouble when it seemed to cross a troubling ethical line with lobbyists, as the *New York Times* reported on September 24, 1976:

> The United States Steel Corporation reported today that it had given President Ford five golfing holidays during his last 10 years in the House of Representatives. The White House declined to comment on the report.

One aide to the President told reporters that Mr. Ford was prepared to answer questions on the subject in his debate here this evening with Jimmy Carter, the Democratic Presidential nominee.

Mr. Ford could attempt to neutralize the point by responding with well-established stories of Mr. Carter's trips, as Governor of Georgia, on airplanes owned by Coca-Cola and Lockheed Aircraft.

And it would be a point that a follow-up September 26, 1976, *New York Times* column discussed:

> Mr. Ford does not even care all that much whether he is re-elected. His vanity is engaged at the moment and he hates to lose. But if he does lose, he will be delighted with his big pension and will play golf and ski and enjoy himself traveling. if he is re-elected, he will be out at Burning Tree with his lobbyist friends playing golf every weekend and one or two afternoons during the week as well. He will ski at Vail, take lots of trips, and make forgettable speeches. Either way, it will be a pleasant…four years for him.

Despite the lapse, President Ford's love of the game was part of his own presidential legacy, often in a humorous way, as he was quoted in the November 6, 1980 edition of the *Oak Leaf*:

> "Betty and I love being in California now that we are residents. Retirement isn't all that bad. As a matter of fact, we recommend it to Jimmy Carter at the earliest possible time," quipped Ford. "Now that I've retired I have more time for skiing and golf. I think I fall down less often and hit fewer spectators on the golf course. Either that, or the press pays less attention now." Ford also included Bob Hope's comments on his golf games, such as, Ford being the only golfer capable of playing four courses simultaneously or losing two golf balls just in the ball washer. "He says that I'm improving, though. He said last round I got an eagle, two birdies, a bull moose and three spectators," said the former President.

He may have left the White House, but golf stayed at his side, as revealed in the November 9, 1976 edition of the *Desert Sun*:

How is Gerald Ford taking it? Easy, and oh so privately, down at the end of Sand Dunes Road, behind high walls, in great comfort. He's taking it Southern California style, like a man of comfortable means and secure future who knows that, suddenly, he really doesn't have to answer personal questions or fret about image anymore. Tucked away for the week in Rancho Mirage, Ford keeps the counsel of his family and a few golfing cronies who might figure in his future plans. He breezes past reporters occasionally with a smile and a joke, en route to the links or back to his secluded villa. And people close to him say he just isn't ready to talk publicly yet about his painful election defeat, or what might have been, or what might be after Jan, 20.

Even after he left office, his golf playing was used in interesting angles. For instance, the March 11, 1980 edition of the *Globe and Mail* had this to say about Ford:

When Gerald Ford competed in the Inverrary Golf Classic last week, he outdrew not only Jack Nicklaus and Lee Trevino but he also commanded larger Florida crowds than Republican presidential candidates Ronald Reagan and George Bush, who were engaged in a different kind of sport.

It's a safe bet that the large galleries were not out to see the former president shot-making. Mr. Ford swings the golf clubs like a man beating a rattlesnake. He has only broken 100 once on the Inverrary links and that was with the help of an unwitting spectator whose shin stopped a Ford shot headed for the Everglades.

The setting was a mere set up to something more political and nostalgic:

The reason the people lined the fairways and applauded warmly was because they want him off the golf course and out on the hustings chasing Mr. Bush and Mr. Reagan. Mr. Ford said before the tournament that if a public demand for his candidacy was forthcoming, he would run.

Although President Jimmy Carter and Mr. Reagan probably are the big winners in the primary here today, Mr. Ford has been generating most of the talk and most of the excitement.

When Gerry Ford left the presidency, the people say, the inflation rate was only 4.8 per cent. Today, under Jimmy Carter, they say, it is running at almost 20 per cent.

And his post-presidential golf games made headlines as they did in the January 21, 1977 edition of the *Desert Sun:*

Hubert Green, Tom Watson and Vic Regalado were the leaders going into the second round of the $200,000 Bing Crosby National Pro-Am today, but not too many people really cared. That's because Gerald Ford, in his first day of retirement, played with Arnold Palmer, and while neither is on a winning streak, not even a modest one, the golfing crowd here was watching the two closely, probably more out of sentiment than curiosity. "I hope he plays well," Palmer said of the now-retired president, "and I hope he has fun so he will want to play again. I think that it is great he is playing in this tournament and as for asking me to be his partner, I'm flattered…"

Ford's golfing helped his post-presidential image, even with his various public stumbles, with the *New York Times* going so far as to call that element *glamour* in an August 31, 1982 article:

He gives expensive speeches. His public appearances, even his love of golf, draw paying crowds, enriching charitable coffers. And he has become a rich man with a rich man's friends and substantial houses.

And when Ford passed away in 2007, it was George H.W. Bush who gave the eulogy on January 2:

On the lighter side, Jerry and I shared a common love of golf and also a reputation for suspect play before large crowds.

"I know I'm playing better golf," President Ford once reported to friends, "because I'm hitting fewer spectators."

He had a wonderful sense of humor and even took it in stride when Chevy Chase had to make the entire world think that this terrific, beautifully coordinated athlete was actually a stumbler.

With Ford, golf polished his post-presidential standing. It placed him in the public eye, golfing at charity events with celebrities, elevating his standing and brand. Golf is a prime gateway for a former president to gracefully and seamlessly enter a non-public sector life: it is the common thread and a door between both worlds and of all of the golfing presidents, Ford managed this feat the best. Golf is neutral ground and in the core of public and private life, of elite power and a more common life, and beyond both the Left and the Right.

Ronald Reagan was not an ostentatious golfer, but his love of the game was well-known even when he was California governor. In an April 12, 1971 article in the *Desert Sun*, Reagan mused about how life in a political office altered his life:

> Occasionally he gets in a golf game with close friends and campaign sup-
> porters, such as William French Smith and Holmes Tuttle, or perhaps
> former Sen. George Murphy. "I was a nut on golf until the horse thing
> 15 years ago," Reagan says, "then I became a vacation golfer. Now I
> guess you could count on two hands the golf games I have in a whole
> year."

Like JFK downplaying his golfing as a response to predecessor Eisenhower, Reagan was optics savvy enough to leverage the sport to his advantage. As one columnist quipped in the *Desert Sun* on July 4, 1978: "Jerry Ford is golfing some-where. Ronald Reagan is organizing everywhere." Thus, while Ronald Reagan was not an avid golfer, he was known to take up the sport and use his charisma out on the green to parlay his message in different ways. As former Senator Bob Dole recounted in his book *Great Political Wit*, Reagan could use the game as his own stage in subtle ways that drove home his message:

> Reagan, like Presidents before and since, also took time to exchange the
> challenges of the Oval Office for those of the golf course. Even when he
> was talking about golf, however, Reagan never strayed far from his po-
> litical message. He once joked that when comedian Bob Hope asked
> him what his handicap was, his response was "The Congress."

Reagan was an athletic man, and took up golf later on in his life, as he played with the elites in Hollywood during his acting career; however, once he became president, he found it difficult to both golf and run a country as authors Peter Hannaford and Charles D. Hobbs in 1994:

> One of Reagan's infrequent golf opportunities—a weekend at Augusta
> (Georgia) National Golf Course with Secretary of State George Shultz

in October 1983—underscored the difficulty of mixing golf and the presidency.

But they noted once he left the White House, he felt liberated enough to return to his quiet love:

When Reagan left the presidency and resumed life in Southern California, he looked forward to more leisure time and even signed up for golf lessons. Nearing eighty, he decided he was now "old enough to learn how to play golf."

Even when he had been diagnosed with Alzheimer's Disease, somehow, golf kept him going as it kept him active and social, as the *Baltimore Sun* noted on February 4, 1996:

On [Ronald Reagan]' 85th birthday Tuesday, House Speaker Newt Gingrich, retired Gen. Colin L. Powell and 500 other people will celebrate the milestone at the restaurant where Mr. Reagan proposed to his wife.

"I plan to play golf with Ronald Reagan on his 85th birthday," said businessman and Reagan friend Lodwrick M. Cook.

And the *Montreal Gazette* also relayed a year later on February 7, 1997:

Ronald Reagan celebrated his 86th birthday yesterday in the same low-key, private way he has lived since being diagnosed with Alzheimer's three years ago.

...After blowing out the candles on a cake decorated with jellybeans, Reagan unwrapped a gift from his staff: golf shoes, in khaki and green suede in honor of his Irish roots.

Later, he headed off to a golf range to drive a few balls before returning to his Bel-Air home for a private dinner with wife Nancy.

For presidents, golf is a form of therapy. For some, it is woven with their job, but for others, it is a different kind of sacred space. For Reagan, it was more private, showing the diverse and flexible nature of the game.

On the other hand, Donald Trump's golf-playing was far more brazen and ubiquitous. He is also the first president to not be just a golfer, but own seventeen golf courses around the world:

- Aberdeen, Scotland

- Bali, Indonesia

- Bedminster, New Jersey

- Charlotte, North Carolina

- Colts Neck, New Jersey

- Doonbeg, Ireland

- Ferry Point, New York

- Hudson Valley, New York

- Jupiter, Florida

- Lido City, Indonesia

- Los Angeles, California

- Miami, Florida

- Palm Beach, Florida

- Philadelphia, Pennsylvania

- Turnberry, Scotland

- Trump World Golf Club, Dubai

- Trump International Golf Club, Dubai

- Washington DC

- Westchester, New York

He is also the first president who has *hosted* a major: The 2017 Women's United States Open was played at the Trump National Golf Club in Bedminster, New Jersey, with Trump among the attendees. Sung-Hyun Park won the event, making her the first golfer to win at a major hosted by a sitting U.S. president.

When it comes to Trump and golf, he is a study of contradictions, and the press would deride him for his golfing. He had beaten another golfer in November 2016 — Hillary Clinton, and it had been a wild four-year ride for him. Like other presidents before him, sometimes the Sport of Presidents was fair game for attack; however, many in the press forget that a president rarely just golfs: it is an extension of the office where rare access to the Commander in Chief is given without lower-level gatekeeping and interference.

The *Washington Post* chided the president's golf playing on March 27, 2017:

Invariably, whenever we look at how much time President Trump spends at the golf courses that bear his name, we incur one of two re-sponses — or both.

1. The president is entitled to time off. 2. Why shouldn't he go to prop-erties that bear his name?

To which the appropriate responses are: (1) He is. However! and (2) For at least one very good reason.

Or, to go into a bit more detail: Can't the president take time off?

Sure! The president, like anyone else, is entitled to some down time. And, of course, the president -- unlike anyone else -- never really gets any. He's always on duty, always available as needed.

When we point out that Trump is playing a lot of golf (as we did on Sunday), the point isn't that he should only be either sitting at a desk making presidential decisions or asleep. The point is that Trump him-self, piggy-backing on the anti-Barack-Obama Republican rhetoric of the past eight years, repeatedly insisted that -- unlike Obama -- he wasn't going to spend time playing golf if he was elected president.

For many presidents, golf was never their "time off." Trump had publicly scolded Barak Obama for being on the golf course, and inevitably, the criticism came full circle.

Because Trump is a polarizing figure, his every move was under scrutiny, and while golf is a presidential pursuit, his ownership of golf courses had been seen as over the top. There were limits and boundaries and expansion of the game requires finesse. The *Financial Times* outlined his dilemma in a July 14 2017 article:

On a Saturday in May when the White House had not released President Donald Trump's schedule to the press, a photo posted to Instagram inadvertently disclosed his location. A club visitor had snapped him at Trump National Golf Club, Bedminster, an acclaimed New Jersey course he opened in 2004.

The tee box on the 16th hole where Mr. Trump was photographed was adorned with signage for the United States Golf Association: Trump Bedminster was making preparations for the U.S. Women's Open, which it hosts this weekend. On Friday morning Mr. Trump confirmed in a tweet that he would be flying in from Paris that afternoon to attend the Open, "their most important tournament".

The luxurious mindset of the 1980s that would have been celebrated a generation before was now under the hot seat:

The tournament, awarded to Trump Bedminster in 2012, should be a moment of triumph for the president, who has long craved the approval of the golf establishment. Instead, his comments about minorities, immigrants and women have led to protests at the tournament against both Mr. Trump and the USGA, the governing body that carries itself as the conscience of the game.

However, the criticism was not universal:

But since Mr. Trump has been in office, attitudes appear to have changed. Peter Bevacqua, chief executive of the PGA of America, the organization of U.S. teaching professionals, voiced his support for Mr. Trump earlier this year. "When you have the president playing golf and saying that golf is a good thing, that's good for the game," he told CNN.

Despite criticism from social groups and three U.S. senators, the USGA has reaffirmed its backing for the tournament being in Bedminster, telling the Financial Times: "We make decisions about where to play based on factors purely related to golf, not who the president is and not based on anyone's personal politics."

When George W. Bush held on golfing in the aftermath of 9/11, many people were not impressed; however, his decision was vindicated indirectly years later when Trump golfed during some national and international quagmires. If the green was understood as an extension of the Oval Office, perhaps the end result would have been different; however, the game was a fair game during the aftermath of Hurricane Dorian, as CNN chastised on September 3, 2019:

> As Dorian grew into a Category 5 hurricane over Labor Day weekend, President Donald Trump played golf. Twice.

> The most common critique of Trump's decision to hit the links was focused on the obvious hypocrisy. And yes, there is that!

CNN had not bothered to look at who was in the golfing party or what had transpired on the course:

> What is more striking -- and damaging as it relates to the overall health of the country -- is that Trump's golfing weekend speaks to how he simply does not see the presidency as a beacon of moral leadership (or leadership of any kind.)

Perhaps there was a positive reason or a more negative one. The Sport of Presidents, when used correctly, sends layers of messages to different groups, and Trump, not having a political pedigree, was less concerned about optics than he was at tweaking the noses of the press.

After all, Trump had golfed with other world leaders during his tenure, as he did with Japanese Prime Minister Shinzo Abe on his tour of Asia in November 2017. For presidents, golfing is a more social way of cultivating deals and alliances on neutral ground in a one-on-one setting. Just as lawyers are present at black-tie affairs should two tycoons decide on a deal, the golf course often serves the same purpose in a less formal and restricted setting.

CNN also frowned at presidential golfing on May 27, 2020:

> In media appearances, posts on social media, and speeches as a commentator and later as candidate for president, Trump said Obama's golfing made it appear he was tired of being president, adding that Obama should have given up golf when his White House term started.

"He may play more golf than any human being in America, and I'm not sure that's good for the President," Trump said in one January 2015 comment.

Those words would come back to haunt Trump throughout his presidency:

The President is now facing his own criticism for golfing twice during Memorial Day weekend as the coronavirus death toll in the United States approaches 100,000 -- an action he defended as "exercise" accompanied by attacks on Obama's golfing habits.

However, despite the golfing whataboutism, there is an interesting element at play: those who criticized a sitting president for his golfing are cursed should he enter the same position. Trump taunted Barak Obama's love of the sport when it was the latter in office. When the shoe is on the other foot, the previous criticisms come in full force. Such was the case in an article in the *Daily Beast* on July 12, 2020:

> President Trump accused his predecessor Barack Obama of not only golfing more (not true) but taking longer to complete a round of golf in a Sunday morning Twitter tirade. Trump, who is estimated to have golfed around 200 rounds in his presidency so far compared to Obama's 100 rounds at the same point, tried to justify his time on the links by calling it a "tiny" bit of "exercise."

And yet, his links to golf could work in his favor, despite the controversy, even before his presidency. A polarizing figure will have a vision that some will reject, but others see as a boon. As the *Financial Times* noted on March 4, 2016:

> Mr. Trump, who is expected to appear at the tournament, has featured heavily in coverage of past Cadillac Championships, landing his Trump-branded helicopter on the course and posing with players on the 18th green.

That he would take time out of his busy campaign schedule to attend a golf tournament reveals much about how Mr. Trump uses the sport to bolster his personal brand. But beneath that, the inflammatory comments that have marked his campaign for the White House have left the golfing establishment questioning its relationship with him.

The article noted that Trump was a powerful force in golf pre-presidency:

> The property tycoon has bet heavily on golf even as the sport's growth has stalled in a developed market such as the US. As well as owning or operating 17 luxury golf clubs around the world, he has managed to

secure the right to host leading tournaments at his courses, such as the Cadillac Championship and the U.S. Women's Open.

And that many in the game credited him for re-aligning the game in positive ways:

> His relationship with golf has not only proved lucrative, it has burnished the Trump brand and brought positive coverage. Jack Nicklaus, regarded by many as the greatest golfer of all time, said last year before Mr. Trump's bid for the presidency took off: "What he's been doing is terrific for the game . . . He brought a new life during a time when the game was struggling."

Trump's golfing rankled his detractors as it brought the entire game of golf to presidential levels, and in a real way, equalized the sport in a subtextual manner. Golf began to merge with the White House as both share a common spirit of competitiveness, strategy, and patient skill. What would the forefathers of presidential golf think had they known their love of the game would carry on decades after their pioneering pursuits? It is often an overlooked question, but one that is important to ponder.

Of all the Republican presidential golfers, the weakest link was Richard Nixon. His golf game was tepid at best, and, worse, he cheated on the course, and frequently. Many saw his penchant to cheat and cover up his mediocre game as a hint of his behavior. However, while he was not a deft golfer, he nevertheless had a genuine fondness for the game.

However, he was Vice President under Eisenhower — the quintessential golf president, and he made an honest attempt at the game as author Jeffrey Frank recounted in his book *Ike and Dick:*

> The vice president was also wise enough in those first months to take up the study of golf, and in the summer of 1953, he worked on his game at the Spring Lake Golf and Country Club in Mantoloking, New Jersey, where he spent weekends with his family. Although he never became fond of the game, he understood its social utility and he was determined to master it. He had even joined the expensive and exclusive all-male

Burning Tree Country Club—Ike's club—in Bethesda, which the news-
paperman Jim Bassett described as "probably the only place in the world
where the President. . . can sit around in his skivvies with his friends"...

Frank also recounted that a self-conscious Nixon would try to work out his
game in private:

Nixon finished third in his foursome and returned the next day in late
afternoon, almost in twilight…when there wouldn't be too many people
on the course. He wanted to get some privacy that way so he could just
play nine holes."

Nixon and Eisenhower golfed together, though Nixon was overwhelmed and
apprehensive, given he was under pressure from a variety of estates: his Commander in Chief boss, the press, and the public.

But golf would be more prominent in his life when he resigned in the face of
Watergate, he found solace in the game as recounted in the May 10, 1975 edition
of the *Desert Sun:*

Richard Nixon has made his first prolonged public appearance in his
home town since resigning the presidency nine months ago, playing 18
holes of golf. "He seemed to favor his leg, but his golf swing looked real
good," said the manager of the Shorecliffs golf course, Jim Perrin. Nixon
played there for three hours Thursday afternoon, accompanied by military aide and Secret Service agents, attracting crowd of about 40 onlookers.

And no detail was too minor to mention:

Nixon used a golf cart "but also did lot of walking," the course manager
said. Nixon is under doctor's orders to exercise moderately to strengthen
his left leg, afflicted with phlebitis condition that brought on two operations, and close brush with death, last fall. "He looked like he'd had
some practice. He hit the ball right down the middle," the course manager said. Nixon can practice at his estate, and has also gotten in some
golf at the Palm Springs home of former ambassador to Britain Walter
Annenberg, which has a private course.

Yet even before his fall from grace, he kept up appearances. Golfing was a key, and he used it in a similar way as his former boss Eisenhower as the November 26, 1971 edition of the *Santa Cruz Sentinel* recounted:

> President Nixon joins celebrities and golfing friends of the late President Eisenhower Saturday for ceremonies dedicating a 140-bed hospital, the start of an Eisenhower Memorial Medical Center in the desert. The hospital is located in the palm desert area, about 120 miles east of Los Angeles, where Eisenhower often came for winter golfing vacations. It is one of a growing number of memorials to the president.

Nixon's golfing had fateful turns with up and comers as well, as author Jules Witcover recounted in 2007:

> …Pat Buchanan…had first met Nixon when the great man had come to play golf with his newspaper's publisher in St. Louis, Richard Amberg. Young Buchanan caddied for Nixon and then left the paper to work for him.

When the Watergate scandal broke, many people used Nixon's golfing methods as a sign that he did partake in shady dealings. Golf was seen as a noble sport that the game would never keep dark secrets away from the American people: it would betray an untrustworthy leader if something dark was happening. Nixon's cheating at the game came back to haunt him.

Yet, it became his therapy post-presidency. As author Mark Updegrove recounted in 2006 in his book *Second Acts*:

> Shortly after his illness, Nixon sought physical rehabilitation through an unlikely outlet: golf. Before becoming vice president, he had tried his hand at the sport a handful of times, yielding less than spectacular results. After becoming vice president, he used it as a means of getting closer to the boss. Ike was an ardent duffer, though his outings with the hapless Nixon proved frustrating for both. Golf suited neither Nixon's lack of physical grace nor his temperament. He saw it as a frivolous waste of time. Now, in need of exercise—and perhaps a diversion—he threw himself into the game with characteristic self-discipline and intensity. With his administrative assistant Jack Brennan as his tutor, he made

strides to break 100, and, playing twice a week or so, gradually brought his scores down.

For Nixon, his relationship with The Sport of Presidents was mixed, complicated, strained, but was a journey for him, nevertheless. It was there during his highs and lows, and his game seemed to improve when he had become more reflective over his past.

Republican presidents are known to golf, and it is no surprise that the sport plays a big part of the mythos; however, Democrat presidents are just as avid golfers, and while it is presented with a different lens, it is no less vital as the following chapter explains.

Chapter Thirteen
A Swing from the Left

In the political sphere, presidents wear their partisan stripes with honor, and yet the sport of golf unified them all. Bill Clinton, Barak Obama, and Joe Biden are all golfers, and for these modern-day Democratic presidents, their use of golf has been more defined than ever before. However, each one has used the sport in very different ways. In short: Obama electrified, Clinton parlayed, and Biden underlined. Each strategy has produced vastly different results and invoked different responses from political rivals.

Like their Republican counterparts, when it was a presidential competition, golf gave an edge at the ballot: Clinton defeated non-golfer Bob Dole, while Barak Obama defeated non-golfers John McCain and Mitt Romney. If you want to be president, it helps if you actually golf.

Of all three modern Democrat presidents, it is President Obama who is most defined by the sport and managed to make both enemies and inroads with the game. He is an excellent and photogenic golfer and images of him playing the Sport of Presidents are stunning. However, as a master of optics, he had been mindful of the pitfalls that plagued other presidents, yet while he shone on the green, he wasn't without his own set of dilemmas.

As a golfer, President Obama knows how to connect to the people. He is a president who used golf to paint a picture of success, but it took some interesting turns, particularly early on in his presidency. It reached international curiosity, and one Irish golfer artist had a link to it all as described in the August 4, 2009 edition of the *Irish Times*:

> Ben Hogan, a study in art if ever there was one, used to have an answer when asked where he got his swing. "The secret's in the dirt," he'd reply, a reference to the time he spent hitting ball-after-ball off the Texas soil — either sand or grass — in his quest to find perfection. His time on

the range was accompanied by a series of divots, almost as if he were digging for oil.

Paul Ferriter also finds his perfection in dirt. He's a golfer, able to play off a single figure handicap, but it's as a sculptor that his quest starts and finishes.

The 41-year-old — born in Donegal, raised in Dublin, and with a studio in the heart of Temple Bar — has earned an international reputation in recent years as one of the foremost sculptors, with a speciality in the golfing form.

… And one of Ferriter's most recent commissions is of an up-and-coming golfer who has been in the international spotlight for over a year. His name? Barak Obama. Word is spreading, you see.

Yet Obama was aware of the unifying and equalizing power of the game, and he leveraged its social factor in his own games. He could connect to more than mere elites. The message did not go unnoticed as it was discussed in the international edition of the *New York Times* on September 8, 2014:

> The recreational approach that he and the president take to the golf course — "It is the only time I can get four or five hours outside, and I don't have the option to take long walks through a city," Mr. Obama said -- infuriates advocates of the Bill Clinton and Lyndon B. Johnson school of golf, in which the green is a lush cell for politicking.

> In a town where government officials, operatives, donors, and lobbyists fantasize about presidential face time, Mr. Obama has bypassed them for a less political group of golf partners. They include Alonzo Mourning, the retired basketball star; Ahmad Rashad, the former Minnesota Vikings wide receiver, who has dated Valerie Jarrett, the White House adviser; pre-White House pals Marty Nesbitt, Eric Whitaker, Mike Ramos, and Bobby Titcomb; and the ESPN personalities Tony Kornheiser and Michael Wilbon.

And his egalitarian approach was a marked contrast to previous presidents:

> When Mr. Obama does play golf with members of the administration, he often passes over cabinet members for relatively low-level -- and low-

handicap — company, including Sam Kass, the president's senior policy adviser on nutrition policy and the Obama family's chef.

However, not everyone was enthralled with his upbeat golf play. One writer in the *Washington Post* sarcastically urged the president to go back to basketball, fearing the worst in a November 13, 2014, Op-Ed piece:

I have figured out what's wrong with President Obama. He gave up basketball and started playing more golf. As a man of roughly the president's age who still plays both sports, I have some insights to offer. Basketball demands all of the qualities that make a good leader. Golf undermines them.

Until fairly recently, Obama played basketball at least once a week, with some pretty formidable competitors, including Reggie Love, a former Duke player, and 6-foot-5 Education Secretary Arne Duncan, who played at Harvard. Since giving up the game, however, Obama has turned to golf, playing nearly 50 rounds in 2013.

This is bad. Let me explain why. Every sport instills and rewards certain personality traits.

However, many readers did not seem to get the humor and were offended by the piece. While Donald Trump often criticized Obama's time out on the green, others were not as upset: after all, presidents golf, and still work even when it seems they are at play.

But how often did he play? As *Golf News Net* noted on March 19, 2017, Obama's golf time during his presidency was a reasonable number of hours:

Former President Barack Obama was frequently maligned by Republican and conservative critics for how often how chose to play golf while in office. Obama, who chose golf as his outlet from the glass cage that is the presidency, had plenty of weekends and vacations to play golf in the eight years he was Commander-in-Chief.

In total, according to CBS News reporter and presidential historian Mark Knoller, President Barack Obama played a total of 333 rounds of golf while President. That means Obama played golf for 1,665 hours of his presidency, which was, officially, 55,008 hours. In other words, Obama played golf for 3 percent of the time Obama was President.

His golfing escapades were often the stuff of legends: he joked that his golf score was *classified* in 2016. In 2015, he posed for a couple's wedding photograph as he was playing golf at the same Southern California course as their wedding ceremony, causing a sensation, but in 2014, his golf game forced another couple to move their wedding to another spot on the same course in Hawaii, though he phoned to apologize. "He was really funny and nice on the phone," they told reporters.

When he was a guest on *Jimmy Kimmel Live*, he recounted a golfing bet he had with actor Bill Murray as ABC News relayed on October 25, 2016:

> "So we thought of a little skit, decided we were going to putt on the carpet, and somebody grabbed a glass, and he won repeatedly," Obama said. "The glass was rigged. Then he's giving me tips about putting. Seriously, he's all, 'I think your right hand's a little too firm.' He took money from me. I paid him $5. Basically the whole visit was a disaster."

> Kimmel asked Obama if it was his money.

> "No, I asked somebody," Obama said.

From meeting golfing legends to trying to get over political impasses, few used golf for an eclectic set of strategies. His golfing left a good impression each time. Yet there were other interesting moments: *NBC New York* reported that even presidents can get snubbed on September 8, 2014:

> President Obama was turned down at several top golf courses in Westchester while he was visiting the area over Labor Day weekend, sources tell *NBC 4 New York*.

> The Trump National Golf Club, the Winged Foot and Willow Ridge were among some of the elite courses that rebuffed the president's request to tee off there, according to several sources who were told about the president's advance team's calls to the club managers.

> Club managers apparently did not want to inconvenience their high-powered and high-paying members over Labor Day weekend by shutting down their courses to accommodate the president.

His post-presidency golfing showcased his social connect in many unexpected, but always relatable ways. One viral video on the golf course made international news, as it did in the December 23, 2019 edition of the *Indian Express*:

A video of former U.S. President Barak Obama holding and kissing a three-month-old baby is internet's new favorite video. Three-month-old Riley and her family were spotted by the former president when he was golfing at Hawaii's Kaneohe Klipper Golf Course in Kailua.

The video, which was shot by Andrea Jones, shows the former president approaching her family and asking "Who is this cutie pie?"

After greeting the family, the former president held the infant before kissing her on her forehead.

Even when he wasn't kissing babies out on the green, he seemed like he was having the time of his life. He looks like he is having *fun,* and his essence resonates with the public out in the open. *People* magazine on December 2, 2020, was in awe with his game:

While the Obamas spent plenty of time in the Aloha State during their eight years in the White House — they traveled there every December into January for the holidays — this is Obama's first post-presidency trip to the state where he was born.

And while he's there, he's partaking in one of his favorite activities: golf.

Obama wore a white polo and blue shorts for the occasion, as well as a wide smile (which has been present on his face since pretty much the exact moment he left office.)

Or he socializes for charitable purposes as the BBC reported May 26, 2017:

Barack Obama, the former U.S. President, enjoyed himself on the golf course in St Andrews during his first trip to Scotland.

He arrived in Edinburgh by private jet on Friday morning ahead of a charity event where he will address philanthropy and business leaders.

The golfing enthusiast then headed to St Andrews, where he played on the Old Course.

He was joined by Sir Tom Hunter, whose charitable foundation had invited Mr. Obama to speak in Edinburgh.

Or to socialize with an A-list golfing partner as TMZ reported on June 6, 2021:

Barack Obama just hit one of the most famous golf courses in the world for a game with some pals ... a group that included one of the most famous NBA coaches around too.

The former President was out at none other than the Pebble Beach Golf Links course Sunday near Monterey, CA ... where he was joined by Golden State Warriors HC Steve Kerr ... who appeared to be his partner (or competition perhaps?) for the day.

Obama built a dream world with his golfing as brought a human touch to it. It is the Sport of Presidents, but presidents are there to connect to their electorate. Of all presidents, he added the most humanity to his game and turned golf into a goodwill rite of passage for the Office. Though there were criticisms, such as the time he was photographed golfing at a Virginia golf course in April 2020 during global lockdowns, his amiable nature, and love of the game have helped weather stormy reactions to his golfing dedication.

Bill Clinton, on the other hand, used golf to polish an image of brilliance, energy, and glamour. The first focus on the newest president was naturally about golf, even if some Canadian reporters suffered from a bout of forgetfulness of that the game was enjoyed by presidents after Eisenhower. Nevertheless, it was seen as a positive sign as it was in the January 20, 1993 edition of the *Globe and Mail:*

Bill Clinton — President Clinton as of this afternoon — is an avid golfer. The evidence is that he will bring to the White House an interest in golf deeper than any president since Dwight D. Eisenhower from 1952 to 1960. His level of interest can be gauged from a letter he wrote Nov. 24 to Robert Trent Jones Jr. at his office in Palo Alto, Calif.

Presidential golf enlightened the newly minted president, according to the article:

The letter is on stationery out of the National Campaign Headquarters in Little Rock, and was passed on here through Jones's office. It's tongue-in-cheek, but shows that Clinton enjoys golf.

"Dear Bob," Clinton addressed the architect, who designed the Chenal Country Club in Little Rock where Clinton has played much of his golf recently. "Why don't you design a par 85 course for the White House lawn? That would signify real dedication to the Clinton administration. Thanks for everything."

The "everything" to which Clinton referred is not elaborated upon, but suffice it to say that Jones has become Clinton's politically correct golf course adviser. Last March, Clinton committed a gaffe by playing at the Country Club of Little Rock, which had no black members. (There is at least one now). Clinton had to clarify his position on the integration of golf clubs.

The press was happy that another golfing president was in the White House. As the *Los Angeles Times* gushed on June 12, 1997, Clinton made golf far more fun than his more somber-golfing predecessor, Bush 41:

> The limousine is actually the fastest, most heavily armed golf cart outside a James Bond movie, and it glides up nearby regularly, seemingly without warning.

> President Clinton alights, then heads for the first tee at Congressional Country Club, frequently with Washington lawyer Vernon Jordan in a five-hour, 80-some-stroke (give or take a mulligan or 12) escape from the White House.

> Many swings have helped straighten out his slice in his second term.

> "Oh, he plays here all the time," says Maxine Harvey, an administrative assistant at Congressional.

> ...[T]hose who have played with Clinton say it's a round of chatter and jokes, broken by yells at his ball.

> "He is probably more sheer fun than anyone I've ever played with--and that's thousands of people," says Roy Neel, president of the U.S. Telephone Assn. in the book "Presidential Lies."

But his penchant for cheating did not go unnoticed:

> "He has a real appreciation [of golf], but he's not a purist."

The liberal mulligans, oft-used metaphorically by his Republican critics, attest to that.

One of his regular golfing companions was attorney Vernon Jordan who was frequently photographed playing with the Commander in Chief. The press made mention of their partnership frequently, calling Jordan First Friend and Friend of Presidents. Their escapades out on the green were newsworthy, as they were in a September 2, 1994 article in the *Boston Globe*:

> Clinton's regular golf partner, Jordan and his wife, Ann, hosted the president and first lady at the Jordans' Chilmark summer home near Quitsa Pond. The small gathering was also attended by Richard Friedman, at whose Oyster Pond home the Clintons are staying.
>
> Friedman, who is not married (but has seen a big increase in marriage proposals since that has been reported), brought his son, Alex, 23.
>
> The president returned to Farm Neck Golf Club yesterday and White House staffers said he shot an 80 -- one stroke above his dream of breaking 80 before his 50th birthday.

It was seen as upscale glamour: while JFK was quiet in his ways, Clinton used golf to convey the same message. Golf defined Clinton's energetic ways and added a human touch in news stories, where the press was always on the lookout for soft political news. The *St. Louis Post-Dispatch* had such a vignette in their August 22, 1995 edition:

> President Bill Clinton knew something was going on when his wife told him that she wanted him to go out and play golf again Monday.
>
> Like many golf addicts, he had turned Hillary Rodham Clinton into a virtual golf widow, playing 91 holes in four days since arriving last Tuesday on a 17-day vacation in Wyoming — while she sat at their vacation residence working on her newspaper column and her book.
>
> As it turned out, Mrs. Clinton had a surprise up her sleeve. For the president's 49th birthday Saturday, she had arranged for pro golfer Johnny Miller to come play with the president on Monday at Jackson Hole Golf and Tennis Club.

The sociability-angle was too hard to resist: folksy glamour was all the rage. The stories were fun, posh, and personal. Gossip columnists had fodder for their copy inches. As Liz Smith dished in *Newsday* on August 22, 1993:

> Because both Ann and Vernon Jordan had just celebrated their birthdays only the week before, the Clintons brought their hosts memorable souvenirs. For Ann, a gold putter with a small gold plaque reading, "For Ann to putt Vernon away!" Vernon received a red tie with sports motifs. Hillary gave Ann a White House photo of the two women together and the president gave Vernon a photo of himself and Vernon on the golf course. On it, Clinton had written: "Thank you for taking all these steps with me."

Clinton's golfing made him look like a premier multi-tasker. As one news report put it in 2002: "He got there about 9 o'clock and stayed until midnight. He was talking golf with Vernon Jordan and discussing Middle East politics like I'd discuss city politics."

Yet his golfing would later be used against him. When one of his golfing companions got in hot water, the golf angle was almost always brought up with derision as it was in *Human Events* on February 19, 2001:

> In this light, the Clintons' demand to install the former President's golfing pat and financial benefactor, Terry McAuliffe, as party chairman seems like a bigger blunder than ever. To many Democrats, he looks like the worst man at the worst time in the worst place.

Vernon Jordan also had his turn in the hot seat during Clinton's impeachment trial over his role in the Monica Lewinsky Affair. The golfing backfired in the optics department, as it did in a *New York Times* article on February 13, 1999:

> [T]here was Vernon Jordan, at first referred to as Mr. Clinton's golf buddy, then dismissed as an almost feudal loyalist, a man tied to the President by some Beltway arrangement of honor and fealty. But Mr. Jordan clarified the relationship. "The President is my friend." And there, again, on screens lining the Senate walls, we caught a fleeting glimpse of affection.

Mr. Jordan reclaimed his friendship from crude public characterizations. He and Ms. Lewinsky both found ways to keep their relationships personal, if not private. At the culmination of this epic social text, their efforts felt almost heroic."

The *Pittsburgh Post-Gazette* also got its digs on February 4, 1999:

And lastly, as the credits start to come up on "Bill Clinton's Impeachment Show," it is only fitting to check in with American Spectator, the conservative magazine that has more to do with the President's troubles than Monica.

Its timely cover carries a drawing of the President's golf pal, Vernon Jordan, the widely respected lawyer and occasional employment agent for specially talented White House interns.

And the *Charleston Gazette* on the same day used a similar snarky framing:

The Lost Platoon crashed another stonewall: Vernon Jordan, the president's golf buddy and Lewinsky's employment agency. Even Starr, grilling Jordan five times, wouldn't indict him.

"I felt I was dealing with a bobby-soxer with a crush on Frank Sinatra," Jordan previously said as he shrugged off lovelorn Lewinsky.

Even Jordan's incessant presidential golfing would be criticized. For instance, when one reporter asked in May 2003, "There was a time when I believed that Vernon Jordan served on every corporate and charitable board in the country. How did he ever find the time for all those photo ops with his pal, Bill Clinton?" Yet despite the turmoil, Jordan remained Clinton's golfing companion, and their circle grew to include another president, as *Politico* reported on August 15, 2015:

As Presidents Barack Obama and Bill Clinton chatted on the first green of a Martha's Vineyard golf course Saturday, it was not two-time major winner Jordan Spieth that held their attention, but Vernon Jordan, the longtime ally of both, who was about to putt.

When Jordan made his putt, Obama fished the ball out of the hole and threw it back to him before making a putt of his own. Clinton then stepped up, took three practice swings, and sank his putt.

Spieth, who is currently high on the leaderboard at the USPGA championships, would presumably have been proud.

The presidents golfed with Jordan, the financier and lawyer, and Ambassador Ron Kirk at the Farm Neck Golf Club, according to pool reports, playing a leisurely foursome ahead of Saturday night's festivities, which will see the Obamas and the Clintons cross paths at Jordan's 80th birthday celebrations.

For Clinton, golf was the way he made deals, showed off his intellectual mettle, and the fact that he *arrived*. Golf was the way to make deals and show the ability to get things done as you have the time of your life doing it. The core of this strategy veered too off course, so to speak, and brought more negative connotations with it. It may explain why both Bush 43 and Obama both scaled back the glamour factor of the game and reset it along the way.

Joe Biden, like most modern-day presidents, golfs, and though his imprint on the game is yet to be seen, there are still some things to be gleaned.

It often didn't matter if he played golf, or entertained his boss's wife when he was away at golf. Michelle Obama had lofty social circles, which included the Bidens as recounted in the *Daily Beast* on February 16, 2013:

The most powerful man in the world is bolting for beautiful Palm Beach to golf with the boys. And he isn't taking wifey.

How many golf and football widows are familiar with this ploy? Wine and dine--then poof, disappear into the golf or football bacchanalian bashes not to be heard from for days.

And what perfect timing. Congress is out for 10 days, Chuck Hagel's nomination is getting a time out while Republicans look for dirt to keep him out of the Pentagon. Time for Air Force One to jet off to South Florida so the president can pick up some pointers from pro-to-the-presidents Butch Harmon and his son, Claude III.

But no moping for Michelle, who really doesn't seem the moping type anyway--more like the hit-the-tricep-machine-at-the-gym type. She's reported to be packing up the girls, heading west to hit the slopes in Aspen along with Smokin' Joe Biden. Yes, Biden. I guess he's a stand-in in more ways than one.

Other times, his recollection of events on the golf course was called into question by critics. The *Intelligencer Journal* on January 24, 2013, had one such case of it:

It's no secret that Vice President Joe Biden has made more than a few gaffes during his political career.

Perhaps his latest is a hard-to-prove comment about a brush with the 2006 school shooting at Nickel Mines. Speaking last week to the U.S. Conference of Mayors in Washington, D.C., Biden made the surprising revelation that he was golfing within earshot of the schoolhouse when a troubled truck driver shot 10 Amish girls, killing five and wounding five.

The remark has triggered a flurry of blog posts from conservative writers, challenging the validity of Biden's account.

The 70-year-old Democrat briefly mentioned the Oct. 2, 2006, shooting as an example of how the "gun violence epidemic" affects towns and cities — big and small.

Biden told the group that it was "pure coincidence" that he was golfing in the area at the time of the tragedy.

"I happened to be literally — probably, it turned out, to be a quarter-of-a-mile (away) at an outing when I heard gunshots in the woods," Biden said. "We didn't know. ... We thought there were hunters."

The vice president didn't specify why he was there.

While he has tried to present himself as a contrast to his predecessor, he is known as an able golfer and has a connection to the sport. *Wilmington News Journal* on June 18, 2014, had revealed not only his talents as a golfer but his association to the sport as well:

Vice President Joe Biden hasn't ruled out a presidential campaign in 2016 but apparently he's planning to play more golf in Delaware. Biden has joined Wilmington Country Club, the same venerable Greenville-area club where Beau Biden, his eldest son and Delaware's attorney general, already is a member.

… But the club's June newsletter listed "Joseph and Jill Biden" as new members — though, unlike others, without pictures. Biden, who has been known to play at Fieldstone in Greenville, is apparently a pretty good golfer. Golf Digest in 2011 had him, with a 6 handicap, as the 29th best in Washington.

Biden's golfing dilemma seems to mimic that of JFK: he wishes to serve as a contrast, even if he has elements in common. It is a conundrum noted in The *Guardian* on April 18, 2021:

> During last year's presidential election campaign, one of Joe Biden's strongest arguments to voters was that he wasn't Donald Trump.

> After engaging in the favorite pastime of the "former guy" with the first trip to a golf course of his presidency on Saturday, he finds that he still isn't.

> …"The course record was still intact," Biden quipped to reporters after an apparently underwhelming round with an adviser, Steve Ricchetti, and his late son Beau's father-in-law Ron Olivere at the Wilmington country club in Delaware.

However, he has also shown his sense of levity on the course:

> But in the same year, as Trump was running for office and Biden was mulling his own political future, he told the then Irish Prime Minister Enda Kenny: "If you want to keep your handicap in golf don't run for president."

> During an average round with Kenny at the taoiseach's home course at Castlebar, County Mayo, Biden was asked how his golf game was going. "Fortunately politics is going better," the then U.S. vice-president replied.

An October 5, 2021 article in *Politico* noted Biden took a page out of JFK's playbook when it came to the sport:

> Biden, meanwhile, is a bit secretive about his golf game.

"He doesn't seem to want people to know he golfs," said Rick Reilly, the author of Commander in Cheat: How Golf Explains Trump. Reilly, a former Sports Illustrated columnist, noted that Biden hasn't posted his score since 2018. He said he's been asking the Biden team for the past year about coming out to the golf course and "they won't even acknowledge he plays."

Yet like Kennedy, Biden is an apt player:

> Despite not taking up the game until later in his life, Biden has a reputation for being a talented golfer. He has long boasted a single-digit handicap (at one point, 6.3) and even ranked 68th in Golf Digest's 2016 tabulation of the top 150 players in D.C. So there was a lot of head scratching among the district's golfers when former Ohio Gov. John Kasich took a remarkably public dig at Biden for being a shitty golfer after he, then-House Speaker John Boehner and Obama all played together in 2011.

The article even went so far as to list Biden's most frequent golfing companions:

Ron Olivere: 5 times
Steve Ricchetti: 4
Hunter Biden (grandson): 2
Ted Kaufman: 2
Jimmy Biden (brother): 2
Jack Owens (brother-in-law): 2
Jim Larkin (director of golf at Fieldstone): 1

How Biden uses the game for the duration of his presidency remains to be seen, but so far, when golfed in Delaware on April 17, 2021, he was more than playing — he contending with reporters' questions from refugee camps to the state of Alexei Navalny. He is on the job regardless of where he is.

There is, however, one modern Democrat president who wasn't a golfer: Jimmy Carter. He was an outlier, and perhaps it may explain why he failed to gain traction with the public: without a familiar humanizing element that displays patience and strategy, Carter had no recognizable anchor, and hence, the public at large could not *read* him. This isn't to say re-election hinged on golf, but to the public, he would be an enigmatic and opaque entity. Golf is a silent *language,* and for a public to make an assessment, there needs to be a reliable form of nonverbal communications with them. Carter failed to seize an opportunity, and hence, lost control of his own story.

Without the sport, Carter had inadvertently impeded his own presidency, and it is an interesting point in history. After all, analysis and comparisons of different presidential golfing styles are nothing new. for instance, the March 20, 1977 edition of the *San Bernardino Sun* had devoted an entire article comparing various presidents: Eisenhower was deemed a "golf addict." Kennedy was touted as a "natural athlete," but Johnson was "not too good." Ford was deemed an "ardent golfer", but Nixon was "awkward on the links."

But the article went on to mournfully decree that "Carter [is] no golfer," and that it was the "end of the presidential golf line" as Carter preferred "fishing, other sports." It also added:

> Dwight Eisenhower was a golf addict. John F. Kennedy was a natural athlete who could swing a golf club with grace and drive a ball with accuracy. Lyndon Johnson liked the game but was not too good at it. Richard Nixon was awkward on the links but has since become a golf enthusiast. Gerald Ford is almost as ardent a golfer as Eisenhower was. But the Presidential golf line has probably stopped with Jimmy Carter. Carter is a softball player, fisherman, auto-racing enthusiast and tennis player of sorts. But a golfer? No way.

The *Santa Cruz Sun* also seemed pessimistic about the future of presidential golf on November 10, 1976:

> The election of Jimmy Carter appears certain to cool the golfing fever that has been around the White House for the last quarter of a century, no more putting on the east lawn. No locker at the exclusive Burning Tree Club in suburban Bethesda, Md. No policy decisions on the first tee. No judging the state of the union by the severity of the president's slice. "Jimmy never took much to golf," a spokesman for the. country's President elect said from Carter's vacation spot off the Georgia coast. "He's more of a softball man. He plays tennis a bit, loves fishing and is crazy about auto racing. But golf? Forget it."

When Ronald Reagan became victorious in the 1980 presidential race, it was already established that he was an able golfer, meaning the presidential tradition would resurrect, and remained firmly in place as of this writing with no signs of abating.

Whether the swing comes from the left or the right, it doesn't seem to matter: the content of political thought may vary, but its structure remains firmly unified: the world's most elite club favors those who can work a club as well as working a crowd.

Chapter Fourteen
The Influence

When we think of influencers and icons of any given sport, we usually think of professional athletes and Olympians to set the trends of their chosen game. They break records and push boundaries aggressively. Very rarely do we take into account outsiders to help shape the sport, and yet with golf, we can clearly see the presidential influence on the game. The influence is more subtle but does not go unnoticed.

But how do U.S. presidents influence the game? How do their contributions and decisions leave a mark on our understanding of golf? How have Commanders in Chief been inspired by the sport, even after they left office? While each president has made an individual contribution to the mystique and meaning of golf, collectively, their unified thread weaves a very different picture. Let's look at each kind of influence in turn.

As an elite group with over a century of global reach, the public message of the game is intriguing. Here, golf is foremost a symbol of active health. The more robust the president, the more predominant golf is to the narrative. Because the president is confined in many ways, there needs to be an elegant method of displaying someone who is spry and always on the move.

For instance, President Taft's love of the game would often make news in mere photographs, as it did in the May 29, 1909 edition of the *Richmond Palladium and Sun-Telegram*. A bold photo of Taft in action was accompanied by a short description:

> This is President William H. Taft, just as he has made a long drive in a golf game. Mr. Taft is an enthusiastic golfer and plays whenever opportunity offers.

Here, the President does not waste a moment to be active and make moves. More intriguing, Taft's golfing entourage were powerful Titans of Industry. The Commander in Chief is always on the move, but in the highest possible circles imaginable. Golf is the way to move within prime circles of influence, and Taft used the game to counter criticisms of his leadership style.

Photographic evidence of his golfing action came up again in the August 1, 1909 edition of *Los Angeles Herald Magazine.* The dynamic images were eye-catching, and once again, it was mere photographs with a succinct caption that drove the message underline the headline *Taft and Sherman Golfing*:

The President can drive — the Vice President can putt.

A dynamic duo of the president and vice president who can socialize together was the simple underlying message. The team of affable Taft and *Sunny Jim* could do more than merely work together, and there was no shortage of articles chronicling Taft's forays on the course. Golf here was more than active: it was fun, dynamic, and a social exercise. In many ways, the game represented dreamy notions of ultimate success: work and play collided together, and it was an escapade and a sign of power during leisure.

The same vein of jovial pursuit could be found over a century later; however, it would evolve to more fascinating symbols of power. For instance, golf is often used as a symbol of suspense. Pre-presidential hopeful Barak Obama used the game for maximum effect on December 28, 2006 ,according to the *Honolulu Advertiser*:

Supporters of possible presidential candidate Barack Obama say they are respecting the Hawaii-born U.S. senator's privacy as he vacations here this week but continue to urge that he seek the Democratic Party nomination.

Obama, who played golf yesterday at the Waialae Country Club, has indicated that he will announce a decision sometime after he returns to the Mainland this weekend.

Here Obama kept his cards close to his chess — even out on the course. He is pondering and mulling his options. As the article went on to note:

U.S. Rep. Neil Abercrombie, D-Hawaii, said he senses that the 45-year-old Illinois senator and Punahou School graduate "knows what he wants to do" but is carefully considering how a 2008 presidential bid would affect his family life.

"I think this has come to him, and I think everybody is projecting on to him their hopes and dreams, the things that they would like to see," said Abercrombie, who was an old friend of Obama's parents and is hopeful he will run.

The optics here were impeccable, and sent a powerful message: to think clearly, a someone worthy of the office must golf. It should be no wonder that Obama handily won the presidency. The story captured the essence of the mystique.

However, this would not be the only article during that period to link Obama to the Sport of Presidents: Rich Miller had written about his encounter with the future Commander in Chief in the December 8, 2006 edition of the *Chicago Sun-Times:*

I've known Barack Obama since he was first elected to the state Senate in 1996, and I've been mostly wrong about him from the start.

In the beginning, I thought Obama had too much "Harvard ambition" about him, but others pointed out to me that his loss to Rep. Bobby Rush in the 2000 Democratic primary seemed to humble him a bit.

Sometime after that loss, I ran into Obama in Jackson Park, a city golf course on the South Side. We chatted pleasantly and he said some brief words to my female golfing companion and we moved on.

Golf was a fateful game that was a stage for things to come:

Afterward, my friend, who is not easily impressed, had a look of pure joy on her face. She talked excitedly about Obama, but I dismissed him as someone who had screwed up his future by running against Bobby Rush. She said I would eat those words one day.

Here we can see the progression of the same basic message: Taft used golf to show the magnetism of his warm personality: Obama upped the message to show he was a natural president on the same platform. Obama understood the nuances of the game and used it ingeniously even before he became a contender.

President Clinton also understood the social dynamics of the game as did President Johnson: Clinton built an alliance with former Canadian Prime Minister Jean Chretien through the game, while Johnson showed his honor and worth in an unusual and clever way. LBJ deftly used the sport to show another side to his personality, as recounted in the 24 February 24, 1966 edition of the *Desert Sun:*

> Lyndon B. Johnson is always a little preoccupied on the golf course but he's anxious to learn. John F. Kennedy had a natural golf swing and loved to trudge the fairways. Dwight D. Eisenhower has always been a fierce competitor on the links and resents an opponent conceding him short putts. These observations were made today by Max Elbin, who as the teaching professional at the famous Burning Tree Club in Bethesda, Md., has played with or given lessons to three of our nation's chief executives. Elbin, the newly-elected president of the Professional Golfers' Association (PGA), was asked to compare the golfing ability of the three presidents after attending the annual dinner of the New York Golf Writers.

The same article went on to give an interesting assessment of LBJ's difficulties in the game, but the flaws, in fact, showed some very positive:

> President Johnson, according to Elbin, hasn't developed the technique of the game yet. "His swing isn't too smooth but he seems to want to learn," Elbin said. "He'll ask a lot of questions about the game and I feel in time he could get his score down. But like all our presidents, he doesn't have much free time to devote to the game.

Johnson's game showed yet another side to him according to Texas Representative Eugen Worley as recounted by author Shep Campbell in 1996:

> Worley liked Johnson's style. "There are three ways you can sort of size up a fellow," Worley observed. "One's playing golf with him, one's drinking with him, and one's playing poker with him. Well, I did all three with [Johnson], and he measured up to every standard that I would ask for in a man. You never caught him cheating. He'd try to bluff the devil out of you; he was like Harry Truman in that respect. But he generally had something to back it up."

Golf is not always meant to cover up the deficits but boldly show humility and flaw. We do not expect perfection but see what the leader does with those flaws, and it is far easier to accept a flawed gold game than a flawed piece of federal legislation. In this way, we can see the president as a whole person, and learn to accept the quirks and shortcomings that come with the package.

Unlike the professional athlete or Olympian whose errors cost awards and impact the legacy, presidential golfing skills have a different set of criteria for people to judge: how does the president handle stress, competition, or defeat?

And what is a mundane reality to a president? The December 29 1984 edition of the *Desert Sun* some fascinating insights from someone who watched many presidents out on the green:

> President Reagan, who flies into Palm Springs today, is the newest keeper of what has become a presidential tradition vacationing in the Coachella Valley. Lyndon Johnson settled a territorial dispute in Palm Springs. Richard Nixon was "not much of a golfer but he played anyway," says Frank Bogert, Palm Springs mayor and official greeter of presidents going back as far as Harry Truman.

Bogert's most telling anecdote was about President Eisenhower:

> …Bogert remembers Dwight D. Eisenhower playing golf at one of the local country clubs. "There were Secret Service all over the fairways and special phones for the press There were telephones all over hell," Bogert said He said the Secret Service came to the club first and interviewed waitresses and other employees.

We often take the images of presidential golfing for granted, yet every grain is vetted and an army of people surrounded the Commander in Chief for even the simplest golf game. While Nixon was not a deft golfer, he too would need a high level of vetting just to play unimpeded. The president never merely goes somewhere: there must be many others who clear the path first, yet it seems seamless once the press comes in to observe and speculate.

And gossip about the happenings on the green, which is rife with fodder. Forget the back tie parties: it is the golf course that has the juiciest of tidbits. For instance, Drew Pearson found a lot of gossip that way that he relayed in the February 14, 1961 edition of the *Madera Tribune:*

Note as Scott McLeod exited as ambassador to Ireland another Scott moved up to lake his place -Scott Peek. His sole distinction: administrative assistant to Sen. George Smathers, Florida golfing partner of President Kennedy and lackadaisical custodian of Senate committee campaign funds. The US. government used to give considerable care to picking Ambassadors to Ireland. But with a son of Erin in the White House, an obscure senate functionary can now qualify. Anyway, whether a Republican or a Democrat, it pays to golf with the President. Even while vacationing at Palm Springs. Ex-president Eisenhower is fretting about whether Kennedy will turn out to be a reckless spender. Between rounds of golf, Ike told friends that Kennedy had better realize you can't spend your way to prosperity. "If he knows what's good for us. we'll pay our way as we go," he told golfing partners.

After decades of being the Sport of Presidents, it should be no surprise that there would be a golf tournament named after the leaders who shared that common thread. Since 1994, the President's Cup pits U.S. men's best golf players against an international team outside of Europe. It is a biennial event with a match play scoring system and is a charitable event. The Chairman of the event alternates from current or former U.S. president to the leader of host nation: Gerald Ford was the inaugural Chairman in 1994, George H.W. Bush in 1996. Other U.S. presidents who served as Chair were Clinton in 2000, George W. Bush in 2005, Barak Obama in 2009, and Donald Trump in 2017. Foreign leaders who served as Chair were Australia's John Howard in 1998, Thabo Mbeki of South Africa in 2003, Canada's Stephen Harper in 2007, Julia Gillard in 2011, South Korea's Park Geun-Hye in 2015, and Australia's Scott Morrison in 2019.

Some of the world's most famous golfers served as captains, including Tiger Woods, Arnold Palmer, Jay Haas, Fred Couples, and Jack Nicklaus. It is a celebration of the Sport of Presidents, weaving the White House, professional athletes, and the public for a charitable cause. It is a crowning touch that has evolved the presidential game into an entity of its own.

Presidential golf has taken the sport into entirely new and intriguing directions: from deciphering codes to world leaders to looking at the regular and new players out with the Commander in Chief, there is no other sport that gives that kind of richness or flexibility. The green is an elite and secret clubhouse of sorts, those in the know look to the course first and foremost for signs and omens of things to come. Modern understanding of golf comes from watching U.S. presidents play the game: the savvier observers understand that the game is a platform and follow the president's lead in turning a game into something far more significant. True players never come back from the game empty-handed: there should be at least a deal made or an impasse resolved. Golf is a safe space and a passage to progress. The presidents who understood the secret world the best made the most of their time playing. The worth of the sport of presidents can be understood by watching how each American leader has leveraged the game as both a tool to get the job done and a signature style of their methods. Golf is not a game for the frivolous or the timid: and we can see how and why U.S. presidents learned to make the most of it.

Chapter Fifteen
The Legacy

When a president can make his own little world on the golf course, it seems this is the leader who can make a nation stronger. That has always been the subtext of the Sport of Presidents. It is a reliable scaffolding to understand both the inner workings of the position in general, but more importantly, to understand the mindset of the Commander in Chief. No other sport reveals so much as golf.

If there is one constant among presidents, it is the game of golf. There may be changes and upheavals with policies and practices, but the game is the backbone of the position. Golf will always be a part of the presidential legacy because it is more than a sport: it is the Swiss Army Knife to the highest office. It is a tool that has multiple tools within it: it allows the president time to think, work out a strategy symbolically, hammer out deals on the green, and let the public know that their leader is multi-faceted and alert. There will never be another sport as fitting or symbolic.

One of the most symbolic displays occurred in 2017 during the President's Cup when Barak Obama, George W. Bush, and Bill Clinton were watching the game together from the sidelines, marking the first time three former presidents were in attendance. As *Golf Digest* noted with awe on September 28, 2107:

> As the start of the 2017 Presidents Cup drew near, three former U.S. Presidents took turns pointing down Liberty National's first hole and shaking their heads. The opening tee shot to what looks like a sliver of fairway guarded by a large pond to the left is daunting enough on the calmest of days. But into a stiff breeze, it now had the ability to make a trio of men who all at one point were the most powerful people on the planet feel powerless.

The presidential hat trick was a happy sight to many:

For one day, Clinton, Barack Obama and George W. Bush blended into the large gallery of fans at Liberty National. Well, as much as three former Presidents surrounded by Secret Service details can blend into a crowd. The three were on hand for the opening ceremony, sitting in a perch beside the first tee, and they were unquestionably the day's biggest stars with the world's best golfers coming by to shake their hands and pose for selfies.

The selfies sent a powerful message: golf brought majesty to the people as it showed the humility of the ones who held office (though it sent another, more overt message as the three former presidents did not meet with then-president Donald Trump). A few months later, *Golf Digest* revealed on January 17, 2018, that Obama and Bush joined the same golf club:

> Houston Astros owner Jim Crane… broke some news regarding two of his course's new members. And not just any two members, but two former presidents.

> "He's a new member and so is George W. [Bush], so I'm very neutral on the politics, so don't get me one way or the other," Crane says in a video shared by Fox 26's Mark Berman. "We invited 43 when he came here to throw out the first pitch, and then we invited Obama. So, we've got both sides of the political spectrum covered."

Yet many who observe presidential golf do not see all there is to the game. As author Marc H. Ellis noted in 2001:

> The President of the United States has become more than a simple physical entity: he has become an icon of the power and vigor of the country. Much public-relations time and effort is spent on making the man in office seem physically perfect and devoid of illness or disability. Countless photographs of the President golfing, jogging, romping on the beach emphasize his robustness and *joi de vivre*.

Authors Joanne Connor Green, Christopher E. Smith, and Daniel M. Shea expressed similar sentiments in 2007:

Finally, the media keep the president in public view, reporting every scrap of available information about the first family's daily life. This reporting is generally framed from a human-interest angle but also includes evaluations of presidential performance. Stories that show the president golfing, jogging, playing with the White House dog, or clearing brush show the human side of the person, and keeping tabs on presidential policy initiatives allows the public to evaluate the chief executive.

However, these observations miss the deeper level: the president isn't just golfing to send a message of personal humanity or health: the leader of the nation is still *working*. A president is never alone on the course: there will always be something to be discussed or logistics to be considered. While it is nice that the Commander in Chief pets the dog or does some yardwork, neither one of those actions has a secondary meaning: they firmly remain a mundane part of life, even for those in the highest office. Golfing, on the other hand, creates its own sphere of influence. There is no other game that allows life-altering plans to be discussed right out in the open in such a convenient way.

Golf is a game of endurance, patience, and skill. There is aim and focus, but it is not a game of open aggression, but often, it can signal a lot more to an entire planet or another head of state a world away. Where every stroke can send a secret message, it should be no wonder why golf is the sport of presidents: there are layers of loud messages to be sent to allies and enemies alike all while quiet deals are made at the same time. It is an intricate mechanism that should never be underestimated or dismissed. It is never just a game, and it is far more complex than mere theatre. Golf strategy and narrative rolled into a single event that tells multiple stories to the press and to an inner circle, and it serves as a Shibboleth to those who need to read the signs.

What lies on the surface may not align with a deeper context. As author Peter Hannaford noted in 2012, President Taft seemed to be a creature of habit when he went on his retreats:

> Taft almost always followed the same daily routine. He played golf in the morning, then had lunch, followed by a nap, then reading or visiting and, after dinner, playing bridge. Taft loved golf and had joined both the Myopia Hunt Club and the Essex Country Club. His friend John

Hammond was his favorite golfing companion. There were other Beverly summer residents he also saw, including Justice Oliver Wendell Holmes and the industrialist Henry Clay Frick.

To the people, this routine signaled stability, and yet, the dynamics were far more complex: John Hays Hammond was a wealthy mining engineer and was appointed a special ambassador by Taft; Frick was a union-busting titan industrialist who defined the steel industry, while Holmes had a very different mindset, and his illustrious, if eclectic company reflected both his strengths and weaknesses. His game reflected his essence.

And over a century later, very little has changed. Pundits and radio hosts debate which president golfed for business and which golfed merely for leisure, with some outlets having golfing *trackers* to keep tabs on whether the current Commander in Chief was spending too much time out on the course, without considering who was in attendance, and what was actually happening. You cannot merely speculate unless you have all of the enigmatic pieces of the puzzle.

Golf may bring gossipy speculation from the press, pundits, and public, but the presidential golf course is its own world where policies are shaped and lucrative access can alter the fortunes of millions of people. Some people spend millions in lobbyist fees, but their influence pales to those who know how to swing and club and know how to gain a direct audience without the usual gatekeepers present.

For a president, there is no such thing as *just* a golf game. Key political alliances are formed if the president appears sincere and honest with his game, but deep rifts can explode should the game come at an ill-opportune time. A single swing can be felt on the other side of the world. The press often forgets to align world events with a president's last golf game, and it is a gross oversight that denies historians, analysts, and the public crucial information and insight.

However, there is no reason why the reader of this book should be so confined: the legacy of the game is well-earned, and there is rich and complex information to be found. Who played with the president, when, where, and how the president played that day can often explain many seemingly enigmatic world events, and with the knowledge, a valuable map emerges.

Golf is the Sport of Presidents for a reason. The club is a key that unlocks a very different world where even play is work. While other nations' leaders also play the game, none of used it to the same level of quiet sophistication as the US, and it explains how such a deceptively simple game has helped transform an Office into a dominate global force, and it is no coincidence that U.S. global dominance was aligned with the sport entering the highest office in the nation. It was never just a key to a different world: but the key to political power itself.

References

Alden, E. (2014). "Obama needs to forget golf and bring back his basketball hustle." *Washington Post,* November 13, washingtonpost.com.

Ambrose, S. E. (1999). *Duty, honor, country: A history of West Point.* JHU Press.

Anonymous. (undated). "Warren G. Harding & Stanley Park." *The History of Metropolitan Vancouver,* Vancouverhistory.com.

Anonymous. (undated.) "Franklin Delano Roosevelt Club Champion Campobello Golf Club Campobello Island, New Brunswick." *Golf Ball Factory,* golfballfactory.com.

Anonymous. (1897). "Mr. McKinley on a Tally-Ho." *New York Daily Tribune,* August 6, page 7.

Anonymous. (1899). "Social and Personal." *Washington Times,* August 7, page 5.

Anonymous. (1906). "Political Notes." *New York Sun,* November 25, page 3.

Anonymous. (1908). "Taft on Golf Course." *Washington Evening Star,* July. 31, page 1.

Anonymous. (1908). "Bourne to be Active with Taft." *Walla Walla Evening Statesman,* November 7, Page 1.

Anonymous. (1909). "Beat 'Em at Golf." *Topeka State Journal,* February 13, page 1.

Anonymous (1909). "William Howard Taft 27th President." *Perth Amboy Evening News,* March 4, page 1.

Anonymous. (1909). "Sherman his partner." *The Washington Sunday Star,* March 28, page 2.

Anonymous. (1909). "Storm Mars Inauguration." *Coeur D'Alene Evening Press,* March 4, page 1.

Anonymous. (1909). "TAFT'S GOLF GAME IN SOAKING RAIN; With Vice President Sherman as Partner, Defeats Gen. Edwards and Capt. Butt in First Administration Game. PLAYED FOR TWO HOURS Storm Comes at Finish of Match, but the President Laughs — Tennis Court Deserted." *New York Times,* March 28, page 3.

Anonymous. (1909). "Athletic Fashions Set by Presidents." *Los Angeles Herald*, April 1, page 6.

Anonymous. (1909). "CROKER VISITS TAFT; THEY DISGUSS GOLF; President Also Shows Interest in the Feats of Orby and Other Horses. CROKER WANTS BET-TING Bookmaking Should Be Legalized, He Declares — Thinks Revision of the Tariff Is Foolish." *New York Times*, April 6, Page 1.

Anonymous. (1909). "Taft as a Golfer." *The Evening Times-Republican*, April 13, page 5.

Anonymous. (1909). "Gossip of National Capital." *Bluefield Daily Leader*, April 23, page 3.

Anonymous. (1909). "Obsequious 'Rubbernecks' Sicken Taft of Golf." *Spokane Press*, May 22, page 4.

Anonymous. (1909). "President Taft Golfing Farm." *Richmond Palladium and Sun-Tele-gram*, May 29, page 2.

Anonymous. (1909). "Taft and Sherman Golfing." *Los Angeles Herald Magazine*, August 1, page 7.

Anonymous. (1909). "TAFT PREPARES FOR TRIP.; His Last Day in Beverly So Occu-pied He Had No Golf." *New York Times*, September 14, page 4.

Anonymous. (1910). "Roosevelt's Transportation Bill." *Washington Herald*, September 27, page 6.

Anonymous. (1911). "Taft Goes Golfing in Georgia, No War in This." *Daily Capital Jour-nal*, March 9, page 1.

Anonymous. (1911). "TILTING AT THE BIG WINDMILL: Senators Cummins and Borah Modern Don Quixotes HAMMERING RECIPROCITY Its Enemies Talk, but Admit Their Defeat Senator Gollinger, the Canadian, Getting Desperate—Pres-ident Taft Not Worrying, but Is Playing Golf." *The Globe*, June 29, page 1.

Anonymous. (1912). "Little Items Thought You'd Care About." *Chicago Day Book*, April 27, pages 29-30.

Anonymous. (1912). "The Presidential Dog Fight." *Chicago Day Book*, April 29, pages 21-22.

Anonymous. (1912). "Sporting Items." *Chicago Day Book*, November 6, page 13.

Anonymous. (1912). "Woodrow Wilson who supported Bryan Silent on Result." *Cairo Bulletin*, June 26, page 6.

Anonymous. (1912). "Merely Politics." *Chicago Day Book*, September 19, page 28.

Anonymous. (1912). "Sporting Items." *Chicago Day Book*, November 6, page 13.

Anonymous. (1912). Untitled Article. *Seattle Republican*, November 8, page 1.

Anonymous. (1914). "Wilson Plays Golf." *Richmond Times-Dispatch*, November 15, page 1.

Anonymous. (1915). "Golf Sport of Presidents — Taft Popularizes Game." *Detroit Times*, July 15, page 6.

Anonymous. (1915). "Celebrated His Birthday." *Riverside Daily Press*, December 28, page 8.

Anonymous. (1916). "Calls President a 'Poor Golfer'; 'Knocks Ball About' Says Expert'." *San Luis Obispo Daily Telegram*, March 21, page 7.

Anonymous. (1918). "Taft Wants More Sport." *The Globe*, January 4, page 9.

Anonymous. (1920). "'Silent Calvin' is a Most Canny Speaker." *Riverside Daily Press*, July 9, page 8.

Anonymous. (1920). "Continues Fires on President's Foreign Policy." *Stockton Daily Independent*, July 20, page 1.

Anonymous. (1920). "Harding Inspect Canal's Operations." *Washington Evening Star*, November 24, page A1.

Anonymous. (1920). "Wilson to See a Movie, Harding Played Golf." *Seward Liberal Democrat*, November 25, page 1.

Anonymous. (1921). Caption. *Great Falls Tribune*, February 13, page 16.

Anonymous. (1921). Caption. *Daily Ardmoreite*, February 14, page 5.

Anonymous. (1921). "President Harding Repairing Golf Bag." *Columbia Evening Missourian*, August 12, page 5.

Anonymous. (1921). "U.S. President Wins Golf Honors." *The Globe*, August 26, page 10.

Anonymous. (1921). "President Harding Club and Wins in Golf Tourney." *Omaha Daily Bee*, August 27, page 8.

Anonymous. (1922). "Golf is Lure of President in Far South." *Cordova Daily Times*, March 10, page 1.

Anonymous. (1922). Caption. *Rock Island Argus and Daily Union*, March 25, page 18.

Anonymous. (1922). Caption. *Washington Evening Star,* May 15, page 13.

Anonymous. (1923). "Harding to Meet British Columbia Official on Links." *San Pedro News Pilot,* June 28, page 1.

Anonymous. (1923). Caption. *Washington Evening Star,* July 8, page 78.

Anonymous. (1923). "The President's Favorite Sport." *Merced Morning Star,* August 28, page 1.

Anonymous. (1924). "Woodrow Wilson at Play Described by Colusa Man." *Colusa Herald,* December 4, page 4.

Anonymous. (1927). "May Start Golf." *Washington Sunday Star,* July 31, page 4.

Anonymous. (1931). "In the Capital." *San Pedro News Pilot,* July 21, page 6.

Anonymous. (1932). "Why Pres. Wilson was a Golf Duffer." *Coronado Journal,* July 13, page 4.

Anonymous. (1934). "New Golf Prexy." *Waterbury Evening Democrat,* November 15, page 12.

Anonymous. (1946). "Eisenhower Modest about Golf Count." *Globe and Mail,* January 14, page 14.

Anonymous. (1952). "Merry-Go-Round." *Madera Daily News-Tribune,* November 24, page 8.

Anonymous. (1953). "Seen a Golfer on the White House Lawn? It's Eisenhower, Keeping His Eye on the Ball." *New York Times,* February 12, Page 18.

Anonymous. (1953). Untitled article. *Dunn Daily Record,* June 17, page 3.

Anonymous. (1953). "Beat Eisenhower at Golf? Envoy Thinks He Could." *Globe and Mail,* June 17, page 4.

Anonymous. (1954). "Weather Keeps Ike from Golf." *Dunn Daily Record,* April 14, page 6.

Anonymous. (1956). "Talk Strays To Bit of Golf." *San Bernardino Sun,* August 23, page 4.

Anonymous. (1959). "Helping the Unemployed." *Detroit Tribune,* May 2, pages 10, 9.

Anonymous. (1959). "Has Ike turned pro?" *Washington Evening Star,* October 18, page 18.

Anonymous. (1961). "Fore! No More?" *Washington Evening Star,* January 4, page A22.

Anonymous. (1961). "Kennedy Lifts Golf Curtain." *Washington Evening Star*, April 4, page A6.

Anonymous. (1961). "Kennedy Relaxes, Swims, Plays Golf in Palm Beach." *Washington Evening Star*, May 13, page A5.

Anonymous. (1963). "'Time Off' Deserved." *San Bernardino Sun*, July 24, page 34.

Anonymous. (1964). "White House Confirms It: Johnson Was Playing Golf." *New York Times*, April 7, page 55.

Anonymous. (1966). "A Golf Pro to Three Presidents Rates Johnson at Bottom of List; Eisenhower Is Called 'Most Serious,' but Kennedy Had 'Best Potential' on Links." *New York Times*, February 25, Page 39.

Anonymous. (1972). "Ex-Senator Prescott Bush Dies; Connecticut Republican Was 77." *New York Times*, October 9, page 34.

Anonymous. (1974). "Golf shot by Ford hits youth." *Globe and Mail*, June 25, page 3.

Anonymous. (1975). "Nixon has Nice Day on Links." *Desert Sun*, May 10, page A2.

Anonymous. (1976). "Carter in West for First Campaign Shot." *Desert Sun*, August 23, page 1.

Anonymous. (1976). "No apology, regret: Ford's golf outings confirmed by lobbyist." *Globe and Mail*, September 24, page 3.

Anonymous. (1976). "President Ford Takes It Easy — in Private." *Desert Sun*, November 9, page 1.

Anonymous (1977). "Ford has a new 'Running Mate'." *Desert Sun*, January 21, page B12.

Anonymous. (1977). "Carter no golfer." *Parade (San Bernardino Sun)*, March 20, page 18.

Anonymous. (1978). "SPORTS ROUNDUP: Golf." *Globe and Mail*, March 16, page 48.

Anonymous. (1990). "SPORTS PEOPLE: GOLF; Membership for Bush." *New York Times*, September 21, page A22.

Anonymous. (1996). "Ronald Reagan will mark 85th birthday but skip party." *Baltimore Sun*, February 4, page 9A.

Anonymous. (1997). "Ronald Reagan Marks 86th with Cookies, Songs, and Golf." *Montreal Gazette*, February 7, page B4.

Anonymous. (1999). "Loose Talk." *Austin American Statesman*, January 3, page A5.

Anonymous. (2001). "THE NATION; IN BRIEF / MARYLAND; Politics Aside, Bush Wins Another Round." *Los Angeles Times*, July 4, page A13.

Anonymous. (2003). "Golfing Bush Fields Reporters' Questions." *Seattle Post-Intelligencer*, May 11, seattlepi.com.

Anonymous. (2008). "Bush says he still fears new terror attacks on U.S." *Associated Press*, May 13, seattlepi.com.

Anonymous. (2009). "Dirty Job but Someone has to Do It." *Irish Times*, August 4, page 23.

Anonymous. (2016). "Golfers in Chief: The Best and Worst Presidential Golfers." *Golf*, February 16, golf.com.

Anonymous. (2016). "President Obama Says His Golf Score 'Is Classified'." *Golf*, February 16, golf.com.

Anonymous. (2016). "Cruz says Trump is Boehner's 'texting and golfing buddy'." April 28, washingtonpost.com.

Anonymous (2016). "Bradley Cooper got belt from Mike Tyson." *Toronto.com*, August 3, Toronto.com.

Anonymous. (2017). "Former Trump campaign manager Corey Lewandowski says President beats Tom Brady at golf." *NBC Sports*, January 25, nbcsports.com.

Anonymous. (2017). "How many times did President Barack Obama play golf while in office?." *Golf News Net*, March 19, gnn.com.

Anonymous. (2017). "Barack Obama enjoys himself on the golf course in St Andrews during first trip to Scotland." *BBC News*, May 26, bbc.com.

Anonymous. (2018). "George H.W. Bush, former president and WGHOF member, dies at 94." *NBC Golf Digital Channel*, December 1, golfchannel.com.

Anonymous. (2019). "Presidents Cup Winners and History." *Golf Blogger*, December 9, golfblogger.com.

Anonymous. (2019). "Viral video: Three-month-old 'cutie pie' grabs Obama's attention at Hawaii golf course." *The Indian Express*, December 23, indianexpress.com.

Anonymous. (2020). "Take a look at the golf courses owned by Donald Trump." *Golfweek*, July 24, golfweek.com.

Anonymous. (2021). "Biden goes golfing in Delaware." *Washington Post*, April 17, washingtonpost.com.

Anonymous. (2021). "BARACK OBAMA AT PEBBLE BEACH HITS THE LINKS WITH COACH STEVE KERR ... Mulligan on First Hole!!!" *TMZ*, June 6 tmz.com.

Anson, R.S. (1984). *Exile: the unquiet oblivion of Richard M. Nixon.* Simon and Schuster.

Arrowsmith, M.L. (1953). "Eisenhower to Welcome Old Friend Today." *Key West Citizen,* February 28, page 1.

Ashburn, L. (2013). "Michelle Obama Stranded by Her Man as Barack Goes on a Golfing Weekend." *Daily Beast,* February 16, dailybeast.com.

Associated Press. (1909). "Taft Enjoying Stay on Ranch." *Pensacola Journal,* October 20, page A1.

Associated Press. (1921). "D.F. Golding at Top of List in Golf Meet." *The San Francisco Call,* August 8, page 3.

Associated Press. (1922). "Harding as One of 'Leading Spirits of Golf'." *Santa Barbara Morning Press*, January 15, page 1.

Associated Press. (1942). "Golf is Given Wartime Go-Ahead by Roosevelt." *Globe and Mail,* April 8, page 16.

Associated Press. (1953). "Golf Cabin Planned for Noted Visitor." *Globe and Mail,* April 4, page 10.

Associated Press. (1961). "Guarding Chief Dangerous Job On Golf Course." *Globe and Mail,* April 6, page 2.

Associated Press. (1963). "Playing Golf, Rose Kennedy Told of Death." *Globe and Mail,* November 23m page 4.

Associated Press. (1971). "Nixon To Help Dedicate New Eisenhower Hospital." *Santa Cruz Sentinel,* November 26, page 8.

Associated Press. (1974). "Ford to Boost Talcott Prospects." *Santa Cruz Sentinel,* April 18, page 5.

Associated Press. (1975). "Enthusiastic Welcome Given President Ford." *Santa Cruz Sentinel,* March 31, page 2.

Associated Press. (1975). "None Could Match Gerald Ford." *Santa Cruz Sentinel,* December 21, page 40.

Associated Press. (1976). "Republican records subpoenaed in President's home town: Ford took golf trips from steel firm's lobbyist." *Globe and Mail,* September 22, page 3.

Associated Press. (1976). "Skeletons in Candidates' Closets." *California Aggie*, September 30, page 8.

Associated Press. (1976). "President-Elect to Cool Golfing Fever." *Santa Cruz Sentinel*, November 10, page 15.

Associated Press. (1977). "Ford Fires, Spectators in Peril." *Globe and Mail*, February 10, page 45.

Associated Press. (1990). "Gorbachev remains strong despite problems: Bush; But deal for Moscow on trade is unlikely." *Montreal Gazette*, May 29, page A11.

Associated Press. (1994). "GOLF Playing to the crowd George Bush, Bill Murray go into gallery at pro-am." *Hamilton Spectator*, February 4, page D4.

Associated Press. (2013). "Golf: Woods, Obama Tee It Up." *Globe and Mail*, February 18, page S4.

Bates, J. (2019). "President Trump Seen at the White House While Hurricane Dorian Approaches the US." *Time*, September 2, time.com.

Beale, B. (1960). "Burning Tree Inaugurates Eisenhower Golf Fellows." *Washington Sunday Star*, October 23, page G2.

Belair Jr., F. (1963). "Guards Can't Dictate to Presidents." *Globe and Mail*, November 25, page 7.

Bell, S. (2003). "Golf Wars." *The Times*, July 17, page 19.

Berhow, J. (2017). "Barack Obama's 11 most memorable golf moments in office, ranked." *Golf*, January 19, golf.com.

Berke, R.L. (1990). "On Right, Signs of Discontent with Bush." *New York Times*, May 1, page A 18.

Beschloss, M. (2014). "The Gang That Always Liked Ike." *New York Times*, November 15, nytimes.com.

Bolluyt, J. (2018). "These Are All of the Presidents Who Loved Playing Golf, Including Donald Trump." *Showbiz CheatSheet*, November 28, cheatsheet.com.

Boylan, P. (2008). "How Good is Barack Obama at Golf?" *Time*, December 31, time.com.

Brandt, L. (2019). "President Trump has abandoned his plan to host the next G7 at his Miami golf resort. Here's a look inside all 16 golf courses he owns around the world." *Business Insider*, October 21, businessinsider.com.

Brannon, J. (2006). "Obama's visit all about golfing, not presidency." *Honolulu Advertiser,* December 28, page 1B.

Breland, Z. (2015). "Obama, Clinton hit the links with Vernon Jordan." *Politico,* August 15, politico.com.

Brennan, D. (2020). "Mike Bloomberg Sponsors 'Trump Cheats at Golf' Billboard in Las Vegas Ahead of Nevada Caucuses." *Newsweek,* February 22, newsweek.com.

Brooks, M. (2021) "Which golf courses does Donald Trump own? Full list of 17 Trump courses, including Aberdeen and Turnberry." *The Scotsman,* January 15, scotsman.com.

Brummett, J. (2021). "Manchin in the Middle." *Arkansas Democrat-Gazette,* June 24, page 25.

Bump, P. (2017). "Donald Trump's golfing is a political problem thanks to Donald Trump." *Washington Post,* March 27, washingtonpost.com.

Burton, J. (2022). "Donald Trump Asked Kid Rock For Advice on Dealing with North Korea." *Newsweek,* March 22, newsweek.com.

Bush, P.S. (1936). "1936 Seen as Big Golf Year in U.S." *Bismarck Tribune,* January 3, page 8.

Bush, G.H.W. (2007). "George H.W. Bush's Eulogy for Gerald R. Ford." Transcript. *New York Times,* January 2, nytimes.com.

Bush, G.W. (2014). *41: A Portrait of My Father.* WH Allen.

Campbell, S., and Landau, P. (1998). *Presidential Lies: The Illustrated History of White House Golf.* Wiley.

Chrétien, J. (2018). "Jean Chrétien's thoughts on a round of golf with Bill Clinton, and the bogeyman Trump." *Toronto Star,* October 14, thestar.com.

Cillizza, C. (2019). "Why Donald Trump Golfing During Hurricane Dorian is a Problem." *CNN,* September 3, cnn.com.

Clarke, T. (2004). *Ask not: the inauguration of John F. Kennedy and the speech that changed America.* Henry Holt and Co.

Coleman, (2012). "Playing Golf with JFK." *History in Pieces,* Excerpt, September 5, historyinpieces.com.

Cormier, F. (1966). *Presidents are People Too.* Public Affairs Press.

Cornwell, R. (1998). "A family that plays to win: The Bush Clan: America's New Dynasty." *Hamilton Spectator,* November 7, page D3.

CNN (2016). "Trump Campaign Defends Controversial Deleted Tweet; Obama to Stump for Hillary Clinton in North Carolina." Transcript. *News Day,* July 5, cnn.com.

Dale, D. (2018). "Mulroney praises bush for his leadership: Former PM speaks of president's wide-ranging successes from acid rain to NAFTA at state funeral." *Waterloo Region Record,* December 6, B2.

Daley, J. (2016). "How Arnold Palmer and President Eisenhower Made Golf the Post-War Pastime." *The Smithsonian,* September 26, Smithsonian.com.

Deakin, J. (1984). *Straight stuff: The reporters, the White House, and the truth.* William Morrow & Company.

Dienst, J. (2014). "President Obama Rejected From Top NY Golf Courses Over Labor Day Weekend: Sources." *NBC New York,* September 10, nbcnewyork.com.

Dowd, M. (1989). "Bush 'Would Encourage' Polish Shift, Aide Says." *New York Times,* August 18, page A6.

Dowd, M. (1990). "A Grim Bush Golfs and Boats as Aides Fret About Image." *New York Times,* August 19, nytimes.com.

Dowd, M. (1999). "Is Bill Clinton finally losing it?" *Charleston Sunday Gazette,* October 24, page 11B.

Dunn, P.R. (2014). "Remembering FDR and His Golfing Legacy." *The Pilot,* April 22, thepilot.com.

Ellis, M.H. (2001). "Edward Said & the Future of the Jewish People." In Aruri, N. H., and Shuraydi, M. A. (Eds.). (2001). *Revising culture, reinventing peace: the influence of Edward W. Said.* Olive Branch Press.

Epstein, J. (2021). "Biden Says First Golf as President Leaves Course Record Intact." *Bloomberg News,* April 17, Bloomberg.com.

Evans, R. and Novak, R. (2001). "Evans & Novak." *Human Events,* February 19, page 10.

Fawcett, W. (1910). "Where Taft Will Play Golf in New England." *Newport Daily Press,* July 16, page 9.

Felber, B. (2018). "George H.W. Bush and a legacy of golfing American presidents." *Pro Golf Now,* December 2, progolfnow.com.

Feloni, R. (2017). "Trump played golf 19 times in his first 100 days — here's why American presidents have been historically obsessed with the game." *Business Insider*, April 29, businessinsider.com.

Ferguson, D. (2018). "George H.W. Bush, former president and WGHOF member, dies at 94." *PGA*, December 2, pga.com.

Finkel, D. (1998). "How It Came to This; The Scandal in 13 acts." *Washington Post*, December 13, page W14.

Forester, M. and Guyon, J. (1989). "Carter Hashed at Breakfast." *Oak Leaf*, November 6, page 6.

Frank, J. (2013). *Ike and Dick: portrait of a strange political marriage*. Simon and Schuster.

Geist, W.E. (1984). "The Expanding Empire of Donald Trump." *New York Times*, April 8, page 6 28.

Gibbs, N., and Duffy, M. (2012). *The Presidents Club: Inside the World's Most Exclusive Fraternity*. Simon and Schuster.

Golden, J. and Chu, D. (2017). "Golfers say Trump has the best game of any president." *CNBC*, October 4, cnbc.com.

Goldenberg, J. and Manfred, T. (2018). "18 photos of U.S. presidents playing golf over the last 100 years." *Business Insider*, August 24, businessinsider.com.

Graham, B. (1971). "War is Hell." *Globe and Mail*, April 9, page 29.

Graham, B. (2017). "Golf Clubs from Richard Nixon." *Billy Graham Library*, December 4, billygrahamlibrary.org.

Greene, R. (1957). "Golfing, Vacationing, and the Presidency." *Washington Sunday Star*, April 28, page A27.

Growald, R.H. (1976). "Ford Sure He Will Beat Carter." *Desert Sun*, page A1.

Hannaford, P. and Hobbs, C. (1994). *Remembering Reagan*, Regnery.

Hannaford, P. (2012). *Presidential Retreats: Where the Presidents Went and Why They Went There*. Simon and Schuster.

Haskin, F. J. (1909). "Pastimes of Presidents." *Los Angeles Herald*, June 20, page 6.

Hauser, M. (2018). "HCHSA Insider: Golf was in George H.W. Bush's blood." *Houston Chronicle*, December 7, houstonchronicle.com.

Heller, K. (2003). "At Augusta and elsewhere, we're better off seeing discrimination for what it is." *Knight Ridder Tribune News Service*, May 1, page 1.

Hensch, M. (2015). "Tom Brady: Trump 'just doesn't lose' at golf." *The Hill*, November 18, thehill.com.

Herskowitz, M. (2003). *Duty, Honor, Country*. Rutledge Hill Press.

Hinton, H. (1953). "How Presidents Get Away From It All; . . . AND SOME OF HIS PREDECESSORS." *New York Times*, April 19, page M26.

Hodges, J. (1997). "FOCU.S.ON GOLF / U.S. OPEN; Capitol Games; Bill Clinton is Only the Latest in a Long Line of Presidents Who Have Had a Passion for Golf." *Los Angeles Times*, June 12, page 6.

Horowitz, J. (2014). "Challenging the president, but only on the golf course." *International New York Times*, September 8, page 1.

Hunt, E.C. (1921). "Will Receive Girl Students." *Washington Herald*, July 22, page 5.

Indap, S. (2016). "Trump drives golfing world into dilemma." *Financial Times*, March 4, ft.com.

Indap, S. (2017). "Trump's Course Divides the Golfing Establishment." *Financial Times*, July 14, ft.com.

James, S. (2003). "Business, pleasure links remain par for the course." *Globe and Mail*, page C6.

Janos, L. (1973). "The Last Days of the President." *The Atlantic*, July, theatlantic.com.

Jenkins, D. (2005). "The Bush Golf Dynasty." *Golf Digest*, October, Vol. 56, Issue 10, golfdigest.com.

Joynt Kumar, M. (2003). "Source material: 'Does this constitute a press conference?' Defining and tabulating modern presidential press conferences." *Presidential Studies Quarterly*, March, Vol. 33, Iss. 1, pages 221-237.

Kaczynski, A. (2020). "Trump golfs during pandemic despite many attacks on Obama for golfing during tragedies and disasters." Transcript. *CNN*, May 27, cnn.com.

Kane, P. (2015). "Obama had a $3 golf bet with House Democrats. Guess who won." *Washington Post*, August 3, washingtonpost.com.

Kelly, T. (2020). "Golfers In Chief: All the U.S. presidents who played golf." *Golf Week*, November 1, golfweek.usatoday.com.

Klosterman, C. (2015). "Tom Brady Talks to Chuck Klosterman About Deflategate (Sort Of . . .)." *GQ*, November 18, gq.com.

Knebel, F. (1961). "Potomac Fever." *Washington Evening Star*, February 23, page A13.

Kranish, M. (1991). "A Fine Line for Bush and Policy on Terror." *Boston Globe*, August 13, bostonglobe.com.

Lalumla, C.J. (1952). "Senator Knows How To Lose." *Santa Cruz Sentinel*, November 18, page 42.

Laurer, M. and Geist, W. (2014). "The President was just outside New York City over Labor Day weekend to attend the wedding of his former Chef Sam Cass and he hoped to sneak in a round of golf." Transcript. *Today*, September 9.

Law, T. (2019). "Report: President Trump Installs $50,000 Golf Simulator in the White House." *Time*, February 13, time.com.

Lederman, J. and Sinco Kelleher, J. (2014). "Obama golf game forces Army couple to move wedding." *PBS NewsHour*, December 30, pbs.org.

Leonard, B. (2021). "Biden plays first round of golf as president." *Politico*, April 17, politico.com.

Lindlaw, S. (2003). "Bush Joins Parents at Family Compound." *Associated Press*, June 12, seattlepi.com.

Luscombe, R. (2021). "'Course record still intact': Biden on first underwhelming golf outing as president." *The Guardian*, April 18, theguardian.com.

Lydon, C. (1976). "U.S. Steel Reports it Entertained Ford." *New York Times*, September 24, page 49.

Macintyre, B. (2001). "Bush follows Clinton down fairway to cheating." *The Times of London*, July 5, page 13.

MacKenzie, C. (1992). "Getting on with the business of being an ex-president." *Globe and Mail*, December 3, page A16.

MacLeod, R. (1960). "Like a Gun-Fight to Blasé Chicago." *Globe and Mail*, November 10, page 7.

Malone, J. (1989). "Bush relaxing with rapid pace of sports on vacation." *Austin American Statesman*, August 27, page A6.

Martin, L. (1980). "Florida Voters Want to See Ford in Race." *Globe and Mail*, March 11, page 11.

McCarthy, N. (2020). "How Many Times Has President Trump Played Golf?" *Statista*, November 11, statista.com.

McIlroy, A. (2000). "Chrétien to hit the links with Clinton." *Globe and Mail*, April 29, globeandmail.com.

McKenna, H. (2017). "Donald Trump loves beating Tom Brady at golf." *Patriot's Wire*, January 26, patriotswire.com.

Melbourne, V. (2001). "Bush Feeling a Bit over Par." *Herald Sun*, July 5, page 32.

Mennella, D. (2022). "PGA Tour lobbying Biden, Congress about 'Saudi Golf League'." *Audacy*, July 30, audacy.com.

Miller, A.M. (2020). "Obama seen on golf course days before Michelle told people to stay home." *Washington Examiner*, April 30, washingtonexaminer.com.

Miller, M. (2006). "Maybe it's right for Obama to run…" *Chicago Sun-Times*, December 8, page 43.

Moore, D. (1953). "Ike to Meet Press Twice Every Month." *Dunn Daily Record*, August 4, page 3.

Moriarty, T. (1966). "SO SAYS PRO LBJ Anxious To Learn Golf." *Desert Sun*, February 24, page 11.

Mouly, F. (2017). "Broken Windows." *New Yorker*, March 31, newyorker.com.

Murphy, W. (2020). "POLS &POLITICS / Union Chips In For Vegas Trip." *New York Newsday*, June 28, page A20.

Mussett, J. (1989). "Golf Style Back from the '50s." *Toronto Star*, July 27, J8.

Myers, A. (2017). "Presidents Cup 2017: For one day, three former U.S. Presidents were simply golf fans." *Golf Digest*, September 28, golfdigest.com.

Myers, A. (2018). "Barack Obama AND George W. Bush recently joined the same golf club." *Golf Digest*, January 17, golfdigest.com.

Nadeau, B.L. (2020). "Trump is Still Falsely Attacking Obama for Golfing More Than Him." *Daily Beast*, July 12, dailybeast.com.

Naughton, J.M. (1976). "Mr. Ford Is Developing the Underdog Role." *New York Times*, August 29, page 127.

Nax, S. (1984). "Truman, Kennedy, Eisenhower Presidential vacations are Coachella Valley tradition." *Desert Sun*, December 29, page A2.

Nichols, H.W. (1953). "Eisenhower Is First Golfer Since Harding." *Dunn Daily Record,* March 5, page 4.

Nossal, F. (1962). "Where Successful Diplomats Play Golf." *Globe and Mail,* March 1, page 7.

O'Brien, E. (1994). "Clinton's blistering sax, glowing golf game." *Boston Globe,* September 2, page 96.

Palmer, E. (2022). "Donald Trump Praised For 'Powerful' Golf Display As Host Teases Joe Biden." *Newsweek,* July 30, newsweek.com.

Parkinson, J. (2016). "President Obama Reads Donald Trump's Mean Tweet on 'Jimmy Kimmel Live'." *ABC News,* October 25, abcnews.com.

Pearl, D. (2017). "Former President Barack Obama Grins While Golfing in His Home State of Hawaii." *People,* March 15, people.com.

Pearson, D. (1961). "It Pays to Golf with JFK." *Madera Tribune,* February 14, Vol. 69, No. 191.

Phillips, R.H. (1961). "Challenges Kennedy: Castro Bitten by Golfing Bug." *Globe and Mail,* March 31, page 1.

Pilkington, E. (2008). "Bush's golf claim angers veterans." *The Guardian,* May 15, theguardian.com.

Powers, C. (2019). "George W. Bush makes his very first hole-in-one at Trinity Forest Golf Club—at age 72." *Golf Digest,* March 20, golfdigest.com.

Reagan, R. (1983). Diary Entry, October 21, reaganfoundation.org.

Reston, J. (1967). "Washington: Golf, Whisky and Mr. Johnson." *New York Times,* September 29, page 46.

Reston, J. (1982). "Happy ex-President." *Desert Sun,* March 5, page A14.

Reston, J. (1988). "Rating Bush: So Far, Not Bad." *New York Times,* December 22, page A23.

Reuters. (1995). "3 Presidential Duffers Hit Some Balls — and Fans." *Seattle Post-Intelligencer,* February 16, seattlepi.com.

Reuters. (1995). "Ahead of the Game Mrs. Clinton Surprises President with Golf Gift." *St. Louis Dispatch,* August 22, page 2A.

Reuters. (2015). "Obama poses for wedding photos with California couple." *Yahoo News,* October 13, news.yahoo.com.

Ribalow, H.U. (1960). "Golf Drawing Israeli Fans." *Arizona Post*, April 15, page 9.

Riechmann, D. (2003). "Presidents Bush Spend Dad's Day Together." *Seattle Post-Intelligencer,* June 13, seattlepi.com.

Riechmann, D. (2003). "Bush Opens Father's Day With Early Golf." *Associated Press,* June 14, seattlepi.com.

Riggs, B. (2016). "Golfers in Chief: The Best and Worst Presidential Golfers." *Golf,* February 15, golf.com.

Ronson, J. (2001). "The Bilderberg Group: Exposed: The secret club of powermongers who REALLY rule the world." *The Mirror,* March 24, page 28.

Rubenstein, L. (1991). "Coach Given Task of Teaching Quayle How to Swing: Golf." *Globe and Mail,* December 7, page A17.

Rubenstein, L. (1993). "Golf: New U.S. President Enjoys Playing a Round." *Globe and Mail,* January 20, Page C7.

Rush, M. (2019). "FDR Golf Club to close due to 'frequent flooding' and lack of profit." *Philadelphia Inquirer,* July 11, inquirer.com.

Ryman, A. (1899). "Addison Ryman's New York Letter." *The Age Herald,* August 20, pages 9, 13.

Schine, C. (1999). "Betrayal, Friendship And Nuance." *New York Times,* February 13, page 19.

Shea, D. M., Green, J. C., and Smith, C. E. (2006). *Living democracy.* Prentice Hall.

Shedloski, D. (2013). "Walker Cup Founder's Descendants Take Pride in Their Link to Match." *USGA,* September 5, usga.org.

Shedloski, D. (2018). "Golf Lineage Ran Deep for President George H.W. Bush." *USGA,* December 1, usga.org.

Sheridan, C. (2020). "Will Donald Trump Ever Play Golf With Tom Brady Again?" *Forbes,* May 24, forbes.com.

Shuey, K. (2013). "Biden Heard Shots From Nickel Mines?" *Lancaster Intelligencer Journal,* January 24, page A1.

Sink, J. (2013). "Bush: Obama Should Play Golf." *The Hill,* September 23, thehill.com.

Sirak, R. (2001). "Presidential Golf." *Golf World,* January 26, golfworld.com.

Skelton, G. (1971). "Political Life Changed Reagan's Work Routine." *Desert Sun,* April 12, page 7.

Smith, J. (2021). "Watch Joe Biden Get "Confused" After His Golf Ball Goes the Wrong Way." *Pro Golf Weekly,* May18, progolfweekly.com.

Smith, L. (1993). "Mr. President Had A Happy Birthday." *New York Newsday,* August 22, page 7.

Smith, M. (1954). "Does Eisenhower Play Too Much Golf?" *Washington Star,* May 30, pages 7, 17.

Starkey, J. (2014). "Joe Biden joins Wilmington Country Club." *The Delaware News Journal,* June 18, delawareonline.com.

Steigerwald, B. (1999). "Don't Judge Esquire by its Cover." *Pittsburgh Post-Gazette,* February 4, page D4.

Stevens, G. (2016). "Obama, PM eager to repair relations." *Waterloo Region Record,* March 7, page A9.

Stewart, J.D.M. (2018). "Fore! The long tradition of prime ministers hitting the links." *Globe and Mail,* April 5, globeandmail.com.

Strege, J. (2018). "George H.W. Bush, 1924- 2018: Golf loses one of its greatest advocates." *Golf Digest,* December 1, golfdigest.com.

Stuever, H. (2003). "Civics Lesson; Who's Who in the Alfalfa Club? Jaime Arauz Knows." *Washington Post,* January 27, page C1.

Suhay, L. (2015). "Obama vs. Trump: Who would win on the golf course?" *Christian Science Monitor,* August 17, csmonitor.com.

Sullivan, G. (1989). *How the White House really works.* Scholastic.

Superintendent of Government Documents. (1973). *Weekly Compilation of Presidential Documents 1973-02-26: Vol 9 Iss 8.*

Superintendent of Government Documents. (1974). *Weekly Compilation of Presidential Documents 1974-09-16: Vol 10 Iss 7.*

Superville, D. (2013). "Tiger Woods joins vacationing Obama for golf round at Florida club." *Associated Press,* February 17, globalnews.ca.

terHorst, J.F. (1978). "Independence Day is a Time for…" *Desert Sun,* July 4, page B12.

Thompson, A. and Sfondeles, T. (2021). "Biden's golf partners, explained." *Politico*, October 5, politico.com.

Updegrove, M.K. (2006). *Second Acts: presidential lives and legacies after the White House.* Lyons Press.

UPI. (1975). "Ford Begins 2-Week Work-Rest Vacation." *Desert Sun*, August 11, page 1.

UPI. (1976). "President Ford A Recipient Of Free Golfing Vacations?" *Desert Sun*, September 21, page A3.

Vanier, C., Field, A., Defterios, J., Tuysuz, G., Cabrera, I., Zain, A., and Stewart, A. (2017). "Donald Trump Has Lunch and Plays Golf with Shinzo Abe; Donald Trump Pledges U.S. Resolve at Yokota Air Base, Japan; Donald Trump Expected to Address Strategies on North Korea with Allied Countries South Korea and China on Asia Tour; Saudi Arabia Intercepts Houthi Missile Attack over Capital Riyadh; Lebanon's Prime Minister Saad Hariri Unexpectedly Resigns, Blames Iran's Influence; New York Marathon has Increased Security after Manhattan Terrorist Attack; New York Marathon will get Drizzle, but Dry Out by Afternoon; Severe Weather and Gusty Winds in Central and Southern Europe will push up into Ireland, England and Scandinavia; Megabrands in South Africa Promote Themselves on Social Media, Paying Instagram Influencers; Facebook Invests in Africa." Transcript. *CNN*, November 5, cnn.com.

Van Natta Jr, D. (2004). *First Off the Tee: Presidential Hackers, Duffers and Cheaters From Taft to Bush. Public Affairs.*

Van Natta Jr, D. (2007). "The Swingingest President Ever." *Time*, June 21, time.com.

Viser, M. (2014). "Activity links commanders in chief: Golf, long a preferred presidential pastime, finds a true fan in the current White House — and some say his game is improving." *Boston Globe*, August 8, page D9.

Watterson, J.S. (2006). *The Games Presidents play: sports and the presidency.* Johns Hopkins University Press.

Weiman, S. (2015). "Golf Remains Obama's Hobby." *Golf World*, October 19, golfworld.com.

Whitney, T.P. (ed.) (1963). *Khrushchev Speaks: Selected Speeches, Articles, and Press Conferences, 1949-1961.* University of Michigan Press.

Wicker, T. (1962). "Kennedy, Eisenhower Hold Quiet Discussion." *Globe and Mail*, March 26, page 8.

Wilson, S. (2011). "'Golf summit': Obama, Boehner team up for win over Biden, Ohio Gov. Kasich." *Washington Post,* June 18, washingtonpost.com.

Winberg, M. (2019). "Why the FDR golf course is going away forever." *Billy Penn,* July 30, billypenn.com.

Witcover, J. (2007). *Very Strange Bedfellows.* Public Affairs.

Youngblood, R.W. (1973). *20 years in the Secret Service; my life with five Presidents.* Simon and Schuster.

Yourish, K. and Lai, K.K.R. (2017). "Trump Tops Obama, Bush and Clinton in Golfing and Private Getaways So Far." *New York Times,* April 28, nytimes.com.